Essays

MW01596164

Editor:
Alan Vardy, Hunter College and the Graduate Center, CUNY

Associate Editors:
Thora Brylowe, University of Colorado
Michael Gamer, University of Pennsylvania and Queen Mary University of London
Alexander Schlutz, John Jay College and the Graduate Center, CUNY

Editorial Board:
Ian Balfour, York University, Canada
Sally Bushell, Lancaster University
Michelle Faubert, University of Manitoba
Anne-Lise François, University of California, Berkeley
Tim Fulford, De Montfort University
Kevin Hutchings, University of Northern British Columbia
Charles Mahoney, University of Connecticut
Rob Mitchell, Duke University
Lynda Pratt, University of Nottingham
Dan White, University of Toronto
Joshua Wilner, City College and the Graduate Center, CUNY
Nancy Yousef, Rutgers University
Sarah Zimmerman, Fordham University

Essays in Romanticism is the journal of the International Conference on Romanticism. *EiR* continues the tradition of its predecessor *Prism(s)* in encouraging contributions within an interdisciplinary and comparative framework. More broadly, we welcome submissions on any aspect of Romanticism, and especially work using emergent or innovative perspectives and approaches.

EiR: Subscriptions

Journal subscription rates can be viewed at https://www.liverpooluniversitypress.co.uk/journals/prices

All members of the International Conference on Romanticism receive the journal as part of their membership. Please see the ICR website for details: http://icr.byu.edu/membership/

How to subscribe:
Essays in Romanticism is distributed worldwide by Liverpool University Press. For ordering information contact:

Liverpool University Press
4 Cambridge Street
Liverpool
L69 7ZU
Tel: +44 (0)151-795 1080
Email: subscriptions@liverpool.ac.uk

Cover and layout design by Mortimer Lebigre.

Typeset by Carnegie Book Production, Lancaster.
Printed in the UK by CPI Group (UK) Ltd, Croydon CR0 4YY.

ISSN 2049-6699 (print) 2049-6702 (online), ISBN 978-1-78962-208-9

Published with the generous support of Hunter College of the City University of New York for the International Conference on Romanticism.

Contents

Important Notice

Liverpool University Press' subscriptions order processing and distribution is now managed by us and not by Turpin Distribution.

This means that all subscriptions related queries should be sent to LUP directly using the contact details below:

Email: subscriptions@liverpool.ac.uk
Tel: 0151 795 1080 (Monday to Friday, 9am-5pm UK time)

We are working hard to ensure that the transition between the systems is as smooth as possible but if you find anything that requires correction or if you have any questions please do not hesitate to contact LUP.

https://doi.org/10.3828/eir.2020.27.2.1

Contributors

William D. Brewer is Professor of English at Appalachian State University in Boone, North Carolina, and the Book Review Editor of *European Romantic Review*. He was the general editor of *The Works of Mary Robinson* (8 vols, Pickering & Chatto, 2009–10), and his other publications include an edition of Regina Maria Roche's novel *The Children of the Abbey* (Valancourt Books, 2016), *Staging Romantic Chameleons and Imposters* (Palgrave Macmillan, 2015), an edition of William Godwin's novel *St. Leon* (Broadview, 2006), *The Mental Anatomies of William Godwin and Mary Shelley* (Fairleigh Dickinson, 2001), and *The Shelley-Byron Conversation* (University Press of Florida, 1994).

Bakary Diaby is Assistant Professor of English at Skidmore College where he teaches courses on Romanticism, the Enlightenment, and Black studies. He is currently working on two book projects, one on the Romantic aesthetics of vulnerability and another on literary critical method from the long eighteenth century to the present. Recent publications have touched on the effacement of Black womanhood in the Romantic period and the perceptions of invulnerability of Black bodies in Romantic-era texts.

Joey S. Kim is a Visiting Assistant Professor at the University of Toledo. She researches eighteenth- and nineteenth-century British literature with a focus on Romantic literature, global Anglophone literature, postcolonial theory, and poetics. More specifically, her research interests converge at the intersection of Anglophone literature and representations of the "East"—how Orientalist subjects and environments take shape in literary, artistic, and cultural objects. Her current book project, *Romanticism and the Poetics of Orientation*, coins the term "poetics of orientation" to describe a poetics newly aware of cultural difference as a site of aesthetic contestation and ambiguity of representation. She has published work in *The Keats-Shelley Review, The Keats-Shelley Journal, The Journal of Commonwealth and Postcolonial Studies, Los Angeles Review of Books*, and elsewhere.

Deven M. Parker is a Postdoctoral Research Associate in the School of English and Drama at Queen Mary University of London. She received her Ph.D. from the University of Colorado Boulder in 2019. Her research has appeared in or is forthcoming from *Studies in English Literature*, the *Keats-Shelley Journal*, and *European Romantic*

Review. She is at work on two monographs, one on telecommunications and mediation in Romantic Britain and the other on the Romantic theater and authorship.

Alice Rhodes is a Ph.D. candidate at the University of York, working on the science of speech production in Romantic literature. Her research interests include: science, technology, and medicine in the literature of the long eighteenth century; Romantic era politics; materialist philosophy; and the works of John Thelwall and Mary and Percy Shelley. She has published on shorthand writing and transcription in the Romantic era and is a contributor to *Romantic Europe: The Virtual Exhibition.*

Leila Walker is an Assistant Professor and Digital Scholarship Librarian at Queens College, CUNY. Prior to joining the Queens College faculty, she served as the Research Associate for *Shelley and his Circle.* Her research interests include the Shelleys and their circle, the digital humanities, the history of science, and the history of the book.

https://doi.org/10.3828/eir.2020.27.2.2

Radical Birdcalls: Avian Voices and the Politics of the Involuntary

Alice Rhodes
University of York

From nightingales and larks, to parrots, starlings, mockingbirds, and gamecocks, the literature of the Romantic period is filled with the sounds of birds. Much critical attention has been given to the way in which Romantic birdsong—the "unpremeditated art" of Percy Shelley's skylark—invokes meditations on poetic production and the relationship or disjunction between animal and human utterances.[1] But what makes a bird's voice different from a poet's and what does it mean for a voice to be "unpremeditated," spontaneous or involuntary? In this essay, I will explore the scientific bases and political implications of birdcalls in the writing of John Thelwall and Percy Bysshe Shelley. Taking Thelwall's infamous allegory of the gamecock, Chaunticlere, and Shelley's less obviously political skylark as my central focus, I analyse the natural philosophy behind their concepts of voluntary and involuntary utterance, and explore their foundations in politically inflected ideas of materialism and Hartleian associationism. For these radical Romantic writers, I argue, the involuntary voices of birds could variously suggest mindless conservative dogmatism or, on the other hand, the spontaneous, and therefore unstoppable, flow of freely spoken radical ideals.

The idea, expressed in Shelley's 1820 "To a Sky-Lark," of unpremeditated bird song as an ideal of unconscious and spontaneous utterance which the human poet both aspires and struggles to achieve has roots in enlightenment discussions of the difference between animal voices and human language. It is in the work of David Hartley, with which Shelley was familiar, that this difference is most explicitly understood in terms of conscious or voluntary, and unconscious or involuntary action.[2] Hartley's 1749 *Observations on Man* begins by theorising that physical vibrations, strengthened by

---

1   Percy Bysshe Shelley, "To a Sky-Lark," in *The Poems of Shelley*, vol. 3, ed. Jack Donovan et al. (Harlow: Longman, 2011), 470, l. 5; See, for example: Angela Leighton, *Shelley and the Sublime: An Interpretation of the Major Poems* (Cambridge: Cambridge University Press, 1984), 121; William Keach, *Shelley's Style* (New York: Methuen, Inc., 1984), 125.
2   Shelley requested a copy of Hartley's *Observations on Man* from Thomas Hookham in 1812, and volume 1 of this book, including Shelley's manuscript annotations, survives in the Pforzheimer Collection of the New York Public Library. See Percy Bysshe Shelley to [Thomas Hookham], 29 July 1812, in *The Letters of Percy Bysshe Shelley, vol. 1: Shelley in England*, ed. Frederick L. Jones (Oxford: Oxford University Press, 1964), 319; Ann Wroe, "Shelley's Good Vibrations: His Marginal Notes to Hartley's Observations on Man," *The Wordsworth Circle* 41, no. 1 (2010): 36–41.

repetition or habit, provide the medium through which humans associate together various sensations and ideas. After introducing these doctrines of vibration and association, Hartley then moves to consider the nature of "automatic and voluntary" muscular motions and their dependence on the preceding theories, suggesting that "association not only converts automatic Actions into voluntary, but voluntary into automatic."[3] Significantly, it is through "a short Account of the Manner in which we learn to speak" that Hartley proposes to demonstrate this theory (105). He explains that new-born babies will only produce sounds when stimulated by pain, but that as the child develops and begins to associate the sounds they make with ideas, the stimuli needed to occasion movement in the organs of speech become increasingly slighter, until "mere Sensations" and "associated Circumstances" will produce the same effect and sounds can be produced voluntarily (105). And it is this process of association which separates human speech from the involuntary utterances of both infants and non-human animals. Hartley writes: "Parrots appear to have less Intellect than Apes, but a more distinguishing Ear, and, like other Birds, a much greater Command of the Muscles of the Throat. Their Talk seems to be almost devoid of all proper Connexion with Ideas" (263). Here, despite the similarities between the vocal organs of humans and birds, particularly imitative birds such as parrots, the birds' failure to associate the motions of the throat which produce sound with the motions of the mind that constitute ideas means that their speech remains involuntary or automatic mechanical action.

Such discussions of the parrot's ability to speak without engaging the mind or will are not, however, exclusive to philosophical or scientific enquiries. For writers of and on the 1790s, involuntary avian voices could have decidedly political resonances. For example, one conservative commentator reflecting on the French revolutionary period in an 1823 *John Bull* article, compares calls for reform to birdcalls. They write:

> It is, we repeat, the repetition—the starling-like cry of REFORM—
> REFORM—which has sounded in men's ears, until they confound the
> meaning and object of it, that *has gained* and *is gaining,* proselytes to a
> formidable and fearful extent.[4]

Starlings, like parrots, can be trained to imitate human speech sounds and were often kept as pets in the eighteenth and nineteenth centuries not for their "own song, but for the beauty of [their] plumage, for [their] docility and aptness in learning to whistle or to speak."[5] Here, as the author uses the chatter of the starling to position the continued spread of reformist ideals in both the 1790s and the 1820s as mimicry

---

3   David Hartley, *Observations on Man, His Frame, His Duty, and His Expectations*, vol. 1 (London: S. Richardson, 1749), 104.

4   "London March 23," *John Bull*, 24 March 1823, 92.

5   James Bolton, *Harmonia Ruralis; or, An Essay Towards a Natural History of British Song Birds* (London: Printed for the author, 1794), 2.

and the repeated "cry of REFORM" as nothing but sound, stripped of "meaning and object," they seek to undermine any claims to rationalism on the part of the reformers. Yet, it is this same mindless and mechanical repetition, the article suggests, which has resulted in the reformist cause spreading quite so effectively. And, as I will go on to argue, this idea that the involuntary quality of bird- or "starling-like" speech renders it uncontrollable and therefore unstoppable, is one which is utilized by pro-revolutionary writers including both Thelwall and Shelley.

John Bull's reformist starling is relatively unique in writing of the period, however, with the majority of talking birds imitating loyalist rather than radical utterances. Helen Maria Williams, for example, in one of her 1795 *Letters* from revolutionary France, recounts an incident in which a parrot is (falsely) suspected of pronouncing counter-revolutionary slogans. Williams describes how a family, living near the German border with their child, Louis, had taught their parrot to repeat "Vive l'empereur" and "petit Louis."[6] Williams continues:

> the bird was denounced, seized as a criminal of importance, and deposited in the house of a revolutionary commissary, where the feathered culprit repeated the guilty sounds. The tidings spread through the city, of the arrest of an audacious counter-revolutionary parrot, who boldly cried "Vive le roi!" (119)

The comedy of Williams's story of the "feathered culprit" soon turns to serious political statement, however, when she informs us that the family who owned the parrot were executed, since the bird could not have formed these opinions independently and must therefore be repeating their words. Throughout the anecdote, Williams dramatizes the way in which imitative birdcalls produce an unavoidable disjunction between sound and meaning. In her reference to the parrot's "guilty sounds," she raises questions about the role of the will in seemingly political statements. Part of the irony which Williams develops in this passage so that "we may smile at the absurdities of our tyrants" comes from our expectation that it is not sounds themselves but the meaning and intent connected with them which is capable of signalling guilt (119). The idea that sounds must be voluntarily and consciously made in order to be pronounced guilty seems to prevail when it is not the parrot, but the owners it mimics who are executed. Yet, in this instance too, Williams draws attention to the revolutionaries' mistaken assumption that sound can be conflated with meaning. While the family taught the bird to praise "l'empereur" and "Louis," neither sound is connected in their minds with the idea of King Louis XVI.

While Williams's letter demonstrates the potentially bloody implications of political parroting, other reformist writers of the 1790s, such as Thomas Beddoes

---

6   Helen Maria Williams, *Letters Containing a Sketch of the Scenes Which Passed in Various Departments of France During the Tyranny of Robespierre* (London: G. G. and J. Robinson, 1795), 118.

and John Thelwall, present such avian repetitions as the antithesis to active political enquiry. Although he is perhaps best known for his medical and scientific work as founder of the Bristol Pneumatic Institute, Beddoes also applied his expertise in the workings of the body and the mind to educational reform. In his 1792 *Extract of a Letter on Early Instruction*, he invokes the idea of the parrot's speech as an analogy for the sort of unthinking loyalism which Beddoes's model of education seeks to counteract. Basing his educational theory, as Mike Jay notes, directly on Hartley's psychology, Beddoes complains that "the habit in the CHILD of hearing and pronouncing certain sounds without any movement of the mind, will dispose the MAN to hear the same sounds with the same vacancy of thought" and continues by sarcastically congratulating the British people on the ability to "repeat our constitutional, much better than our church, catechism, and in the same parrot style" and asking "why should we distress ourselves with doubt, or puzzle ourselves with enquiry?"[7] For Beddoes, as for Hartley, to speak like a parrot is to produce sound without any interaction from the associative "motions of mind" which are required for mechanical response to stimulus to develop into voluntary speech. Furthermore, as he compares the voices of parrots to the mindless repetition of constitutional and church catechisms, he aligns the involuntary with conservative loyalism, suggesting that utterances that are unconnected with conscious will stand in the way of political enquiry and, consequently, reform. The radical orator, poet, and elocutionist, John Thelwall makes a similar point in the closing address to his first series of *Tribune* lectures, delivered in the spring of 1795, following his arrest and acquittal for high treason the previous year. He tells his audience:

> Sentiments of genuine liberty must be the result of laborious reasoning, and must spring from deep-rooted principles. To be efficacious they must be felt and understood, and not like the babbling of a parrot, who repeats words, but understands not the meaning they are intended to convey.[8]

Thelwall, like Beddoes, uses the "babbling" of parrots as a model of communication which, in its lack of connection to ideas, is wholly unsuitable for the cause of liberty. For reform to be successful, he argues, it must be founded on voluntary reason—the "laborious" motions not just of the tongue, but of the mind.

It is not a parrot, however, but a gamecock, that is at the centre of Thelwall's most extensive investigation of the politics of involuntary action. In 1793, Daniel Isaac Eaton printed a report of a speech by Thelwall, which he titled *King Chaunticlere;*

---

7   Mike Jay, *The Atmosphere of Heaven: The Unnatural Experiments of Dr Beddoes and his Sons of Genius* (New Haven: Yale University Press, 2009), 55–6; [Thomas Beddoes], *Extract of a Letter on Early Instruction, Particularly that of the Poor* (n.p., 1792), 4, 18.

8   John Thelwall, *The Tribune, a Periodical Publication Consisting Chiefly of the Political Lectures of J. Thelwall*, vol. 1 (London: Printed for the author, 1795), 336.

or, The Fate of Tyranny, in which Thelwall argues that loyalty to authority is purely mechanical habitual motion which can be overcome by mental volition. He suggests that it is:

> natural to all animals, after they have been long used to perform certain actions in consequence of any particular stimulus, applied either to the sight or any other of the senses, to continue those actions, by mere mechanical impulse, whenever the usual objects are presented, without ever reflecting what it is they are doing: just as men, of base and abject minds, who have long used to cringe and tremble at the names of kings and lords, for fear they should be clapped in bastiles [*sic*], or turned out of their shops, continue to cringe and tremble, when neither shops nor bastiles happen to be present to their imaginations.[9]

He then goes on to demonstrate the physiological bases for this claim with an anecdote about Chaunticlere, a tyrannical gamecock who Thelwall, overriding what he considers to be his own loyalist mechanical and involuntary impulses, or "aristocratic prejudices," beheads in an overt allegory of regicide (34). Chaunt, however, continues to move after death, exhibiting "the continuance of the habitual muscular motion after (by means of the loss of his head) he was no longer capable of knowing what he was about" (35). This thus supports both Thelwall's materialist assertion that thought is a property of the brain and proves that certain physical actions are entirely automatic and unconnected with rational thought or deliberate mental action.

A number of critics, including John Barrell and Michael Scrivener, have explored the way in which the Chaunticlere anecdote demonstrates Thelwall's belief that mechanical and involuntary action is suitable only for passive loyalism and that, consequently, reform can only take place through the intervention of voluntary reason.[10] However, the 1793 speech is not the last we hear of Chaunticlere. When the bird reappears in Thelwall's satirical 1795 poem *John Gilpin's Ghost; or, The Warning Voice of King Chanticleer*, "written before the late trials" but not published until after Thelwall's acquittal, he does not only run around, quite literally, like a headless chicken, but speaks.[11] And the message which he delivers is distinctly radical. The poem, which satirises Thelwall's loyalist antagonists, or "treason-hunters," and their anxieties about the prospect of a radical uprising, ends with a spectre of impending

---

9   John Thelwall, "King Chaunticlere; or, The Fate of Tyranny," in *Selected Political Writing of John Thelwall*, vol. 1, ed. Robert Lamb and Corinna Wagner (London: Pickering & Chatto, 2009), 34.

10   John Barrell, *Imagining the King's Death: Figurative Treason, Fantasies of Regicide, 1793–1796* (Oxford: Oxford University Press, 2000), 106–7; Michael Scrivener, *Seditious Allegories: John Thelwall & Jacobin Writing* (University Park: Pennsylvania State University Press, 2001), 114.

11   John Thelwall, "John Gilpin's Ghost; or, The Warning Voice of King Chanticleer," in *Selected Political Writing of John Thelwall*, vol. 1, ed. Robert Lamb and Corinna Wagner (London: Pickering & Chatto, 2009), 103.

revolution appearing before them in the form of the (still headless) Chaunticlere. Thelwall concludes:

> And still he spurn'd and flapp'd his wings
> And shook his spurs of steel,
> While trembling joints and haggard looks,
> The council's fears reveal.
>
> For thus prophetic flow'd the strain
> That pierc'd each wond'ring ear [...]
>
> "My crowing speaks the envious light
> That soon must clear the sky;
> For *kingcraft's, priestcraft's night* is past.
> And *Reason's dawn* is nigh.
>
> "In me behold the fate to which
> All tyranny must bow,
> And those who've long oppressed the poor
> Shall be as I am now."
>
> He spoke—they would have stopp'd his voice,
> And kept him close confin'd;
> But ah! He 'scap'd their anxious care,
> As flits impassive wind.
>
> And still he stalks abroad, the fate
> Of tyrants to display;
> *Nor can the Attorney General's self*
> *The headless spectre lay.*[12]

Robert Lamb and Corinna Wagner suggest that the Chaunticlere of *John Gilpin's Ghost* has "thrown off his habitual behaviour to recite a republican message."[13] Yet, although Chaunticlere here heralds the dawn of "Reason" which is at odds with both unthinking action and the habitual rule of "kingcraft" and "priestcraft," Thelwall does not necessarily suggest that the gamecock is himself acting as a result of voluntary mental powers. After all, as Thelwall is keen to emphasize, Chaunticlere still kicks out and flaps his wings and, of course, as he remains headless is still presumably

---

12 Thelwall, *John Gilpin's Ghost*, 111–12.
13 Lamb and Wagner, *Selected Political Writing of John Thelwall*, vol. 1, 102.

incapable of "knowing what he was about."[14] Yet, contrary to the model of mechanical loyalism which Thelwall sets out in the original *King Chaunticlere* anecdote, the radical republican content of the gamecock's speech in *John Gilpin's Ghost* is not undermined by the potentially involuntary nature of its production. In her discussion of Thelwall's lectures, Mary Fairclough argues that "Thelwall attempts to correct the condemnation of instinctive behaviour."[15] Similarly, in resurrecting his decapitated gamecock for *John Gilpin's Ghost,* Thelwall suggests that there may, in fact, be a role for instinctual and involuntary action in radical politics, and in this case, he does so through a reworking of his own apparent criticisms of involuntary action as presented in *King Chaunticlere.* Far from preventing the communication of republican beliefs, it is precisely the spontaneity of the bird's utterance that enables the effective spread of its message. Just as Chaunticlere's involuntary movements could not be stopped, even in the severing of body from mind, the automatic voice of "the headless spectre" cannot be restrained or silenced.

But what has changed to allow Thelwall to turn the gamecock's mechanical movements into a channel for radical spoken utterance? Yasmin Solomonescu has explored the way in which Thelwall's materialist philosophy "sought to reconcile David Hartley's doctrine of mental associations with a radical faith in individual agency" and, I would argue, it is in the two Chaunticlere tales that Thelwall dramatizes his reworking of Hartley's theory, allowing him to find a place for "individual agency" in his model of involuntary action, and consequently, a place for involuntary action in his model of radical reform.[16] At the centre of Thelwall's engagement with Hartley is the distinction between stimulus and control. Whereas Hartley's theory suggests that all movements of the mind which constitute conscious thought are mechanical reactions to vibrations that originate outside the body, Thelwall emphasizes that external force is not enough to bring about either life or mind. In his 1793 *Essay towards a Definition of Animal Vitality,* for example, Thelwall argues that "life in the animal is that state of action (induced by specific stimuli upon matter specifically organized), by which the animal functions, or any of them, are carried on."[17] Here, the ability of matter to organize itself prior to stimulus being applied is a key condition of life.

Thelwall goes on to develop this idea and apply it to the functions of the mind in his experimental "series of politico-sentimental journals," *The Peripatetic,* published later the same year. He presents his conviction that "memory and reflection are something more than impassive vacancy—or immaterial suggestion—that they dwell

---

14   Since the gamecock is still without a head, it presumably still has no access to conscious thought which, as Thelwall makes clear in *King Chaunticlere,* is supposed to be an action of the brain.
15   Mary Fairclough, *The Romantic Crowd: Sympathy, Controversy and Print Culture* (Cambridge: Cambridge University Press, 2013), 108.
16   Yasmin Solomonescu, *John Thelwall and the Materialist Imagination* (Basingstoke: Palgrave Macmillan, 2014), 28.
17   John Thelwall, *An Essay Towards a Definition of Animal Vitality* (London: Printed for the author, 1793), 39.

in the vital essence of the blood, and are modifications of that susceptible organization, without which the breath that gives us life were nothing."[18] Here, neither the "impassive vacancy" of mechanical impulse, nor the "immaterial suggestion" of divine influence are the sole cause of thought. Stimuli, as Thelwall makes clear, only work if matter is both organized and responsive or "susceptible." Matter, therefore, has agency. External forces are not able to direct or animate matter; they can only awaken its inherent latent potential. Thelwall's model therefore allows for mental action to be physical and spontaneous, yet not reliant on external power or influence, and this is what enables him to change the way he characterizes the involuntary in the Chauntclere tales. When the gamecock returns in the later tale, he has no access to conscious reason, but his newfound radicalism is neither habitual behaviour nor obviously the result of any external influence or control. Although Chaunticlere does not think for himself, neither is he merely parroting. The bird's revolutionary prophesies therefore present an alternative both to action governed by voluntary reason and to "mere mechanical impulse." His speech is involuntary, yet entirely autonomous. Thelwall is therefore able to reclaim the involuntary for the side of reform, presenting a defiant vision of spontaneous and unstoppable radicalism.

In 1801, after years of government persecution and a resulting hiatus in his political activity, Thelwall re-entered public life as teacher of elocution. Although his new elocutionary career was calculated to distance him from his more overtly radical past, Thelwall's writing on elocution continues to demonstrate the same fundamental belief in liberty that is at the heart of his political writing. And it is again through reference to the voices of birds that Thelwall's elocutionary texts suggest that unconscious utterance is not only suitable, but perhaps even necessary for spreading a reformist message. In keeping with his own preference for delivering both political and elocutionary lectures from only the sparsest of written outlines, spontaneity was an important tenet of Thelwall's elocutionary theory. As with the Chauntclere tales, Thelwall draws a precise picture of the exact function of the will in perfect spontaneous elocution, advocating a model of speech which is unconscious, yet not habitual. Judith Thompson argues, for example, that for Thelwall, "the perceptive organ is not simply a passive recipient of external impulses but an active, co-creating, co-responding instrument."[19] And while Thompson notes how critical it is for Thelwall to present speech as an active process, respondent to but uncontrolled by "external impulses," Julia Carlson observes that "fluent and melodious speech, however, demanded not a more conscious application of the will—not a more deliberate direction of energy toward the vocal and enunciative

---

18   John Thelwall, *The Peripatetic*, ed. Judith Thompson (Detroit: Wayne State University Press, 2001), 255.

19   Judith Thompson "Re-sounding Romanticism: John Thelwall and the Science and Practice of Elocution," *Spheres of Action: Speech and Performance in Romantic Culture*, ed. Alexander Dick and Angela Esterhammer (Toronto: University of Toronto Press, 2009), 29.

organs—but a restoration of the primary sympathy between mind and body."[20] Thus, Thelwall's elocutionary theory presents a model of speech in which the voice is neither externally directed, nor consciously willed—it is truly spontaneous.

As a result, discussions of "Spontaneous Oratory, with specimens of unpremeditated Elocution" featured regularly in his lectures and, as with many aspects of his elocutionary system, were illustrated by quotation from the work of other writers.[21] It is with an extract from Laurence Sterne's *Sentimental Journey* concerning a starling that Thelwall demonstrates his enduring belief in the power of unconscious utterance. The passage opens with Sterne's protagonist, Yorick, attempting to convince himself that "the Bastile is not an evil to be despised," when he is interrupted by a caged starling repeating the words "I can't get out."[22] The bird's speech affects Yorick in such a way that he instantly pledges himself to liberty, noting that: "mechanical as the notes were, yet so true in tune to nature were they chaunted, that in one moment, they overthrew all my systematic reasonings on the Bastile" (3). Here, the "mechanical" babble of the starling does not just suggest the bird's own absence of reason, but it also has the power to dispel Yorick's conservative "systematic reasonings" in favour of more spontaneous and unconscious pro-liberty sentiments. While the starling has clearly been taught these words (presumably by the person who tamed it), they are also "true in tune to nature." The sound "I can't get out" is, in one sense then, habitual repetition, yet it is also, albeit by coincidence rather than association, representative of the bird's mental ideas. Furthermore, although Sterne's original text was written in 1768, Thelwall's quotation of the passage in the decades following both the French Revolution and his own 1794 imprisonment on a charge of high treason, unavoidably engages with a specifically radical figuring of the Bastille as a symbol of tyranny. Again, Thelwall turns the involuntary voices of birds to radical political ends, in this case reaching further than the bird's own speech, to awaken corresponding sentiments in the listener.

How political, then, is the "unpremeditated art" of Shelley's skylark, and how might the bird's song signal more than an aesthetic ideal of free-flowing poetry? Whereas Thelwall believes in the power of "spontaneous oratory" and "unpremeditated elocution" to enact reform, Shelley consistently returns to the idea of unconsciously inspired poetry as a catalyst for political action. In *A Defence of Poetry* (1821), for example, it is the composition of poetry which "is not subject to the control of the active powers of the mind" and which "has no necessary connection with consciousness or will" which turns poets into legislators.[23] And, significantly, Shelley's

---

20   Julia S. Carlson, *Romantic Marks and Measures: Wordsworth's Poetry in Fields of Print* (Philadelphia: University of Pennsylvania Press, 2016), 270.

21   *York Herald*, 23 January 1802, 2.

22   Laurence Sterne, "The Captive," in *Selections, &c., for Mr. Thelwall's Lectures on the science and practice of Elocution*, ed. John Thelwall (York: Printed for the author, 1802), 2–3.

23   Percy Bysshe Shelley, "A Defence of Poetry," in *The Major Works*, ed. Zachary Leader and Michael O'Neill (Oxford: Oxford University Press, 2003), 699.

poets are "the influence which is moved not, but moves" (701). Poetry with the power to effect change cannot be either commanded by internal will or moved by external force. In illustrating this distinction between truly spontaneous poetry and poetry which, although unconscious, is simply conveying the words of someone or something else, Shelley turns to the idea of the "mock-bird." Making the case for John Milton as "the third epic poet," after Homer and Dante, Shelley compares him to several writers who he has discounted as members of his poetic triumvirate (692). He writes:

> For Lucretius had limed the wings of his swift spirit in the dregs of the sensible world: and Virgil, with a modesty that ill became his genius, had affected the fame of an imitator even whilst he created anew all that he copied; and none among the flock of mock-birds, though their notes are sweet, Apollonius Rhodius, Quintus Calaber Smyrnaeus, Nonnus, Lucan, Statius or Claudian have sought even to fulfil a single condition of epic truth. Milton was the third epic poet. (692)

For Shelley, then, the most effective and socially powerful poetry of the kind he advocates throughout *A Defence of Poetry* cannot bear any marks of mimicry. Even poems which he considers largely original, such as the work of Virgil, do not meet his criteria for epic poetry if they are presented as imitations. And, when Shelley characterizes the series of poets who follow the tradition of Homer as a "flock of mock-birds," he does not simply argue that their work is derivative in terms of style and subject but suggests that their automatic, imitative method of composition prevents their poetry from fully realizing its socially beneficial potential. "Mock-bird" poetry is inimical to the idea of "epic truth," which Shelley defines earlier in *A Defence of Poetry* as "that principle by which a series of actions of the external universe and of intelligent and ethical beings is calculated to excite the sympathy of succeeding generations of mankind" (692). Poetry which is capable of conveying "epic truth," then, is writing which does not draw solely from the internal "intelligent" consciousness of the poet, nor is it simply a mechanical and automatic reaction to external action. Rather, Shelley suggests, poetry which hopes to effect change by eliciting a response in "succeeding generations of mankind" must be produced by a combination of external and internal factors. For Shelley, neither voluntary, active composition nor involuntary and reactive repetition are satisfactory means of producing poetry.

Furthermore, I would like to argue that Shelley also presents Lucretius as a kind of mock-bird or starling in this passage and that in doing so he emphasizes his argument that poetry should be created unconsciously but not mechanically. When Shelley writes that "Lucretius had limed the wings of his swift spirit in the dregs of the sensible world" he figures the philosopher-poet as a bird who has been trapped with birdlime, an adhesive substance which was used to capture songbirds. And, Shelley suggests, it is specifically "the sensible world"—that is a world composed purely of physical matter capable of being apprehended in its entirety by the senses—which has trapped Lucretius, transforming him from a wild bird into a caged one. As Sharon Ruston has noted, Lucretius' first century BC poem *De Rerum Natura*, known in English as *On the Nature of Things*, was widely considered in the Romantic period to be a work of "materialism and atheism."[24] While, as Ruston also demonstrates, the materialist features of Shelley's own poetry draw strongly on Lucretius' philosophy of eternally cycling matter, in this passage from *A Defence of Poetry*, Shelley suggests that *De Rerum Natura* ascribes too much power to the physical and external universe to the detriment of individual "spirit" (140). Dante, by comparison, is able to hold the position of "the second epic poet: that is, the second poet" by behaving involuntarily and instinctively, without losing his autonomy (692). As Shelley writes, Dante's "very words are instinct with spirit" (693). Thus Shelley, like Thelwall before him, cannot support a version of materialism or of poetic utterance that completely denies the role of "individual agency," an inherent power or "spirit" which can be influenced and stimulated by external forces or unconscious instinct, but never "moved" or controlled.

Shelley's disparagement of "mock-bird" utterances is not limited to his arguments about poetic power in *A Defence of Poetry*. The mock-bird also carries the same explicitly political connotations for Shelley as the parrot does for Beddoes and Thelwall. For example, in "The Witch of Atlas," written in the summer of 1820, around the same time as "To a Sky-Lark," Shelley aligns imitative birdcalls with unquestioning loyalty to the monarch. The poem describes a dream, instigated by the eponymous witch, in which:

> The king would dress an ape up in his crown
> And robes, and seat him on his glorious seat,
> And on the right hand of the sunlike throne
> Would place a gaudy mock-bird to repeat
> The chatterings of the monkey.—Every one
> Of the prone courtiers crawled to kiss the feet
> Of their great Emperor when the morning came,
> And kissed—alas, how many kiss the same![25]

Here, as Shelley figures the king and his courtiers as a monkey and a mock-bird respectively, he recalls Hartley's analysis of the voices of apes and parrots. When Shelley describes the replacement of the king with a monkey dressed in robes and a crown, he satirically undermines both the legitimacy of the monarchy and the authenticity

24   Sharon Ruston, *Shelley and Vitality* (Houndmills: Palgrave Macmillan, 2005), 49.
25   Percy Bysshe Shelley, "The Witch of Atlas," in *The Major Works*, ed. Zachary Leader and Michael O'Neill (Oxford: Oxford University Press, 2003), 506, ll. 633–40.

of its supporters. Although Hartley, as we have seen, argues that "Parrots appear to have less Intellect than Apes," he suggests that the "chattering" of monkeys cannot be equated with human speech, either, due to the "Narrowness of their Memories, Apprehensions, and Associations" (261). Once again, then, we find an example of the imitative call of the mock-bird signifying nothing more than the mindless repetition of a ruler's words, which are themselves lacking in meaning.

Shelley's alignment of imitative birds with loyalist and monarchist dogmas brings us back to his claim for Milton as the "third epic poet," distinct from the "flock of mock-birds" (excepting Dante) who preceded him. As Shelley emphatically notes in the 1820 preface to "Prometheus Unbound," "the sacred Milton was, let it ever be remembered, a republican and a bold inquirer into morals and religion."[26] Milton, then, is neither a poetic nor a political mock-bird, but rather an example for Shelley of the suitability of spontaneous poetry for carrying republican and reformist messages. Milton notably describes his own act of poetic composition as "unimplored" and "unpremeditated" in Book IX of *Paradise Lost* when he writes:

> If answerable style I can obtain
> Of my celestial patroness, who deigns
> Her nightly visitation unimplored,
> And dictates to me slumbering, or inspires
> Easy my unpremeditated verse:[27]

Although Milton here makes no reference to the role of individual agency in his portrayal of "unpremeditated verse" (he has, after all, been dictated to), Shelley uses this passage from *Paradise Lost* in *A Defence of Poetry* to support his argument that "the mind in creation is as a fading coal, which some invisible influence, like an inconstant wind, awakens to transitory brightness; this power arises from within" (696–7). Shelley thus refigures the external direction of the Muse as a stimulus which does not dictate, but awakens, an unconscious yet inherent power in the poet.[28] It is by these means that Shelley redefines Milton's "unpremeditated verse" as truly spontaneous utterance and this can also be seen in his borrowing of Milton's term to describe the bird's song in "To a Sky-Lark."[29]

---

26   Percy Bysshe Shelley, "Prometheus Unbound," in *The Major Works*, ed. Zachary Leader and Michael O'Neill (Oxford: Oxford University Press, 2003), 231.

27   John Milton, *Paradise Lost*, ed. Alastair Fowler (Harlow: Longman, 2007), Book IX, ll. 20–4.

28   It is worth noting that Thelwall too turns to Milton as a model for spontaneous and uncontrolled oratory and poetry in his elocutionary writings, proposing that "we shall learn to applaud that free spontaneous flow of oratorical period, which the versification of Milton so transcendently [sic] displays." John Thelwall, *A Letter to Henry Cline Esq on Imperfect Developments of the Faculties Mental and Moral, as well as Constitutional and Organic and on the Treatment of Impediments of Speech* (London: Printed for the author, 1810), 165.

29   Shelley misquotes Milton's phrase "unpremeditated verse" as "unpremeditated song" in *A Defence of Poetry* (697). This error, I would argue, is revealing as it both suggests a greater degree of spontaneity

The skylark can be read not only as a model for poetic production, then, but as an archetype of radical autonomy. Shelley begins "To a Sky-Lark" with the lines:

> Hail to thee, blithe Spirit!
> Bird thou never wert,
> That from Heaven, or near it,
> Pourest thy full heart
> In profuse strains of unpremeditated art. (ll. 1–5)

And continues to describe the bird's song as:

> Like a Poet hidden
> In the light of thought,
> Singing hymns unbidden,
> Till the world is wrought
> To sympathy with hopes and fears it heeded not (ll. 36–40)

Like Chaunticlere, the bird's voice is both unpremeditated and unbidden—it is not voluntary, but neither does it rely on any external power to command it. And, like Thelwall's use of Sterne's starling, the lark's unbidden song allows its listeners to access similarly unconscious or unheeded "hopes and fears" which expand the world's capacity for sympathy. Finally, pre-empting the arguments he would go on to make in *A Defence of Poetry*, Shelley reflects that if the poet were able to speak with a voice as simultaneously involuntary and "unbeholden" as the bird's, "the world should listen then—as I am listening now" (ll. 48, 105). The voice of the lark, in its unpremeditation, its autonomy, and its demand to be listened to therefore becomes a model for the process of spontaneous utterance by which a poet's words become apt to stimulate action in the listener. The lark's unconscious song, despite its lack of "proper Connection with ideas," is thus far from being the habitual repetitions of a loyalist parrot or mock-bird, suggesting instead the power of the involuntary to effect radical change.

It is perhaps no coincidence that Thelwall's and Shelley's radical and spontaneous birdcalls appear in the mid-1790s and the early 1820s respectively, or that the *John Bull* author who denounces the "starling-like cry of REFORM" looks back from the latter of these decades to the former. As Kenneth Johnston notes, these two moments, surrounding "Pitt's Gagging Acts in 1795" and "Sidmouth and Castlereagh's Six Acts of 1819" presented a "double defeat" for the reform movement.[30] The lead-up to and aftermath of the 1795 and 1819 Acts, which extended the definition of treason,

---

("verse" brings to mind a far greater level of conscious structuring and composition than "song") and may also indicate that Shelley is thinking less of *Paradise Lost* than his own "To a Sky-lark" (a poet's "unpremeditated art" is verse; a bird's is song).

30   Kenneth R. Johnston, *Unusual Suspects: Pitt's Reign of Alarm and the Lost Generation of the 1790s* (Oxford: Oxford University Press, 2013), 4.

further proscribed supposedly seditious publications, and limited the scope and size of public lectures and meetings, also represent perhaps the two most significant crisis points for freedom of expression in the Romantic period. It is not surprising, then, to find these two pro-liberty writers imagining a form of utterance which is impossible to restrict, a version of the voice which is essentially uncontrollable and unstoppable. While Thelwall thus turns Chaunticlere's speech into the herald of revolution, for Shelley "[t]he most unfailing herald, companion, and follower of the awakening of a great people to work a beneficial change in opinion or institution, is poetry."[31] But the radical orator or poet must not simply imitate the bird's call—they must produce their own instinctual song.

---

31   Shelley, *A Defence of Poetry*, 700–1.

https://doi.org/10.3828/eir.2020.27.2.3

Sensitive Plants and Senseless Weeds: Plants, Consciousness, and Elizabeth Kent

Leila Walker
Queens College, City University of New York

When a group of researchers recently tested the effects of anesthesia on plants, they made a remarkable discovery: when trapped in a glass container filled with ether gas, or when drinking from roots soaked in lidocaine, the plants appeared to lose consciousness.[1] The fronds of a pea plant stopped swaying and drooped. A Venus fly trap ignored the sensation of a simulated bug crawling across its leaves. *Mimosa pudica*—often called "the sensitive plant" in reference to the way it appears to withdraw from human touch, and known to Romanticists for Percy Bysshe Shelley's poem of the same name—did not withdraw. When the drugs wore off, the plants appeared to regain consciousness. Plants, the popular press was quick to report, might have a consciousness to lose.[2]

Implicit in the incendiary language of the popular press is a crude working definition of consciousness. Consciousness, in the sense used here, is not just the capacity to respond to external stimulus, but the capacity to withdraw—and to be vulnerable to the loss of the capacity to withdraw. Consciousness, so defined, is not only inherently intersubjective: it is confirmed through a particularly violating intersubjective relationship. Plants can respond to touch, and they can be forced to endure touch against what might best be called their will.

These experiments, and the popular reports on them, provoked a swift rebuke from dissenting scientists. Devang Mehta, a biologist at the University of Alberta, replied at length to the question in the *New York Times* headline: "Sedate a Plant, and It Seems to Lose Consciousness. Is It Conscious?" "The answer," Mehta wrote, "unreservedly,

---

1   K. Yokawa, T. Kagenishi, A. Pavlović, S. Gall, M. Weiland, S. Mancuso, and F. Baluška, "Anaesthetics Stop Diverse Plant Organ Movements, Affect Endocytic Vesicle Recycling and ROS Homeostasis, and Block Action Potentials in Venus Flytraps," *Annals of Botany* 122, no. 5 (October 2018): 747–56, https://doi.org/10.1093/aob/mcx155.

2   JoAnna Klein, "Sedate a Plant, and It Seems to Lose Consciousness. Is It Conscious?" *New York Times*, 2 February 2018, https://www.nytimes.com/2018/02/02/science/plants-consciousness-anesthesia.html; Jason Daly, "What Sedated Plants Can Teach Scientists About Anesthetizing People," *Smithsonian.com*, 6 February 2018, https://www.smithsonianmag.com/smart-news/how-knocking-out-plants-solving-mystery-anesthesia-180968035/.

is 'no.'"[3] He pointed out that the actual report made no claims about "consciousness," although he also recalled that a previous study by the same lead scientists had been widely criticized for relying "on superficial analogies and questionable extrapolations." While he could find little fault, "scientifically and methodologically speaking," with either experiment, he expressed concern that a collective uncertainty about what "consciousness" means and how one might test for it might lead non-scientific readers to misinterpret behavior that "*looks to us*" like the behavior of consciousness. The language of the popular press, he lamented, inevitably turned to the language of analogy and anthropomorphism.

Perhaps unsurprisingly, Mehta's plea for scientific accuracy in popular reports had little effect. Not long after, when a different study found that a plant's genetic response to touch hindered its growth, popular headlines claimed that "plants don't like touch," and they might even "hate" it.[4] Green thumbs were warned to back off. While presumably hyperbolic, these reports assign to plants not only an awareness of their environment, but actual feelings about that environment and the kind of care (or harm) inflicted on them by others. But as Danny Chamovitz, Director of the Manna Center for Plant Biosciences at Tel Aviv University, argued, awareness does not necessarily indicate self-awareness, or consciousness. "We care about plants," he writes, "do they care about us? No."[5]

It would be easy to read this back-and-forth as a case of weary scientists battling a stubbornly ignorant public. But such a reading would neglect the way that genre affects how we ask, and answer, these questions. It is not so much, I would argue, that it is *wrong* to suggest that plants are conscious, or feeling, or caring; while these claims may be unsupported by existing scientific evidence, they reveal the gap between a scientific and literary approach. The implicit questions that lurk behind the popular headlines have less to do with chemistry, or genetics, or the ability to feel without a brain, than they do with the responsibility we, as humans, might bear toward beings that are simultaneously so like us and so unlike us. As František Baluška, one of the lead authors of the 2018 study of the effects of anesthesia on plants, replied when a journalist asked if his findings indicated that plants are conscious, "No one can answer that because you cannot ask them" (Klein). One imagines a sly wink, but Baluška's answer does more than just side-step the question: it reminds us of the limits of our own capacity to infer from observation when our perspective is limited by our own embodiment. Perhaps even more telling is what Baluška *does not* say. Baluška

3   Devang Mehta, "Plants Are Not Conscious, Whether You Can 'Sedate' Them or Not," *Massive Science*, 14 February 2018, https://massivesci.com/articles/plants-conscious-intelligence-movement-sedate/.
4   La Trobe University, "Plants Don't Like Touch: Green Thumb Myth Dispelled," *ScienceDaily*, 17 December 2018, www.sciencedaily.com/releases/2018/12/181217105853.htm; Joe Hinchliffe, "Plants Hate Green Thumbs—Science Backs Hands-off Gardening Approach," *The Sydney Morning Herald*, 16 December 2018, https://www.smh.com.au/national/plants-hate-green-thumbs-science-backs-hands-off-gardening-approach-20181215-p50mgl.html.
5   Daniel Kolitz, "Are Plants Conscious?" *Gizmodo*, 28 May 2018, https://gizmodo.com/are-plants-conscious-1826365668.

does not say, "No one can answer that because *plants cannot tell us*"—the failure, if it is a failure, lies in our capacity to *ask*.

The questions raised by these experiments are not new. But the concerns revealed by this experiment strike me as particularly Romantic in the way they attempt, and largely fail, to navigate questions of subjectivity, sociality, and the limits of our capacity to know the other. And, in fact, a recent scientific article criticizing the field of "plant neurobiology" accused its proponents of engaging in a "new wave of Romantic biology."[6] The rhetoric surrounding the effects of anesthesia on plants illuminates three key philosophical points that blur scientific and poetic modes of inquiry, which I will address here: first, the social sensitivities and insensitivities that define consciousness; second, the limits of our human capacity to meaningfully observe beings that are fundamentally unlike us; and third, the ethical considerations raised by differences that cannot be bridged by either science or language. These concerns, I argue, are central to Elizabeth Kent's *Flora Domestica* (1823) and *Sylvan Sketches* (1825), both botanical works that double as literary anthologies. Kent, long a neglected figure in literary studies, has received some scholarly attention of late for her contributions as a botanist or for her role in the intertextual sociality of the Cockney Circle—but rarely both together. However, severing Kent's literary project from her scientific project erases the gap between literary and scientific knowledge that her work exposes. In a time when the distinction between science and poetry could frequently blur, Kent's works navigate these boundaries with particular attention to the kinds of relationships each entails. In so doing, I argue, she advances an ethics of care attuned to consciousnesses beyond our understanding, rooted in the contested borderland between scientific and poetic knowledge.

1. Sensitive Plants

The ability of certain plants to move, to respond to external stimulus, has been studied for centuries, and experiments on this responsiveness tend to reflect the concerns of their historic moment. A 1925 study by Jagadis Chandra Bose found that plants, specifically the sensitive plant, can both feel, and feel inebriated; the *New York Times* headline announced that plants "like alcohol."[7] In 1969, Robert M. Maniquis was inspired to write his study of sensitivity and plant symbols in Romanticism by experiments conducted by H. L. Armus, psychologist at the University of Toledo, which suggested that plants, like Pavlov's dogs, could be conditioned.[8] Ken Yokawa, František Baluška, and the team of scientists responsible for the 2018 experiment on the effects of sedation

---

6   Lincoln Taiz, Daniel Alkon, Andreas Draughn, Angus Murphy, Michael Blatt, Crhis Hawes, Gerhard Thiel, and David G. Robinson, "Plants Neither Possess nor Require Consciousness," *Trends in Plant Science* 24, no. 8 (1 August 2019): 677–87, https://doi.org/10.1016/j.tplants.2019.05.008.

7   "Scientist Says Plants Can Feel Like Humans; Sir Jagadis Chandra Bose Declares They Sleep, Shrink, Bend and Like Alcohol," *New York Times*, 9 November 1925, https://www.nytimes.com/1925/11/09/archives/scientist-says-plants-can-feel-like-humans-sir-jagadis-chandra-bose.html.

8   Robert M. Maniquis, "The Puzzling *Mimosa*: Sensitivity and Plant Symbols in Romanticism," *Studies in Romanticism* 8, no. 3 (Spring 1969): 129–55.

on plants were inspired in part by the work of the nineteenth-century scientist Claude Bernard, whose experiments between 1868 and 1878 demonstrated that application of ether could render *Mimosa pudica* unresponsive.[9] Building on William T. Morton's 1846 discovery of anesthesia, Bernard hypothesized that plants and animals shared a common sensitivity to changes in their environment, and concluded in his 1878 *Leçons sur les phénomènes de la vie communs aux animaux et aux végétaux* that "What is alive must sense and can be anesthetized, the rest is dead."[10] At the end of the eighteenth century, experiments testing the effects of Galvanism on a variety of plants (the sorts of experiments concerning the power of animation in dissected frogs that in part inspired *Frankenstein*) produced mixed results.[11] Botanist and author Maria Jacson suggested that these Galvanic experiments might be refined to more definitively resolve the question of plant sensitivity, and noted that "[t]he effect of the electric fluid is similar, when administered to excess, in its power of destruction, both to animal and vegetable life; and, on the contrary, according to late experiments, electricity, carefully made use of, has been found salutary to the individuals of each kingdom" (18). Common to all these experiments is the notion that plants might share with us not only particular sensitivities, but also vulnerabilities. To be sensitive, to be alive, to be animate, is to be open to the violence of scientific experiment.

These experiments also reveal an anxiety, particularly acute in the late eighteenth and early nineteenth centuries, that distinctions between life forms (or even between life and death) might be too close for comfort. The Linnaean system relied on observable, taxonomic distinctions to name and categorize species, working off strict analogies to group like with like. As Theresa M. Kelley has argued, "Romantic era frictions between the ambition to name and classify all plants and a strong suspicion that plants might 'confound' any system devised to accomplish this goal, together with its middle position among the kingdoms of nature, made botany an epistemic minefield."[12] Yet, as "eighteenth-century experimentalists gathered evidence that some species had traits that resembled species that belonged to other kingdoms, it became more difficult to insist on" their separation (7). Plants, especially the sensitive plant, destabilized taxonomic order (5).

Maria Jacson's *Sketches of the Physiology of Vegetable Life* (1811) explicitly invites readers to take up the question, still apparently unsettled, "Whether vegetables are possessed of faculties which may entitle them to a place amongst the animal orders of

9   Ken Yokawa, Tomoko Kagenishi, and František Baluška, "Anesthetics, Anesthesia, and Plants," *Trends in Plant Science* 24, no. 1 (January 2019), https://doi.org/10.1016/j.tplants.2018.10.006.

10   Quoted in Alexandre Grémiaux, Ken Yokawa, Stefano Mancuso, and František Baluška, "Plant Anesthesia Supports Similarities Between Animals and Plants: Claude Bernard's Forgotten Studies," *Plant Signaling & Behavior* 9, no. 1 (January 2014), https://doi.org/10.4161/psb.27886.

11   [Maria Jacson], *Sketches of the Physiology of Vegetable Life* (London: John Hatchard, 1811), 16–18; D. C. Willdenow, *The Principles of Botany and of Vegetable Physiology, Translated from the German* (Edinburgh: William Blackwood, 1805), 223.

12   Theresa M. Kelley, *Clandestine Marriage: Botany and Romantic Culture* (Baltimore: Johns Hopkins University Press, 2012), 6.

the creation?" (6).[13] Drawing analogies between the movement, form, and appearance of various plants and animals, Jacson boldly claims, "By attentive observation of the motions of vegetable life, we discover in plants an appearance of volition equal to that which manifests itself in various tribes of the animal creation" (11–12). The exact phrasing of this claim deserves attention, because it illuminates both the power and the limitations of scientific observation. Although Jacson insists that scientific experimentation had not yet provided a satisfactory rationale for distinguishing plants from animals, she upholds the foundational principle that "attentive observation" will, eventually, yield at least the "appearance" of an answer. Yet Jacson's linguistic waver is revealing: can science infer volition from the *appearance* of volition? And can scientific methodologies reliant on the power of observation go beyond the observable?

Maria Jacson was not alone in questioning the dependability of traditional boundaries between plant and animal in the classification of life forms, although most scientific literature of the time dismissed the apparent motion of plants as "merely external," and not evidence of a vegetable will.[14] But while the science of plants struggled with strict distinctions between forms, writing about plants likewise blurred generic boundaries, and these generic crossings allowed authors the freedom to explore more extreme analogies. In Erasmus Darwin's *The Botanic Garden* (1791), anthropomorphized (and often highly sexualized) plants expressed sensation, desire, emotion, and agency in the poetic sections, while extensive footnotes provided scientific explanations for the poetic imagery. Lush botanical illustrations, some of which extended on fold-out pages beyond the limits of the book, underscored the implicit connection between scientific and artistic aesthetics, while suggesting the uncontainable excess generated through such crossing. As Dahlia Porter has trenchantly argued, Darwin's mode of interweaving scientific notes and poetry, while keeping the two forms visually distinct on the page, effectively plots "a relationship between these realms without conflating their functions or goals."[15] Darwin mobilizes textual form to negotiate (and transgress) the boundary between scientific and poetic knowledge.

The generation following Darwin adopted, in various ways, elements of this composite form, experimenting with combinations of poetry and scientific notes. In Charlotte Smith's *Conversations Introducing Poetry* (1804), for example, children learn the names and characteristics of various plants through dialogue with a patient mother who intersperses bits of poetry throughout her lessons. In Smith's posthumously published *Beachy Head* (1807), the long poem is followed by extensive and exacting scientific notes. Frances Arabella Rowden's *A Poetical Introduction to The*

---

13   I follow Kelley's spelling of Jacson's name.
14   *The New Royal Encyclopedia*, ed. William Henry Hall (London, [Preface dated 1788]), III, "Sensitive Plant," quoted in Maniquis, 137. Maniquis treats the body of scientific literature surrounding the sensitive plant at length in comparison to the plant's literary function.
15   Dahlia Porter, *Science, Form, and the Problem of Induction in British Romanticism* (Cambridge: Cambridge University Press, 2018), 98.

Study of Botany (1801) treated botanical themes in poetry without Darwin's overt sexualization, and the eighth edition of Priscilla Wakefield's *Introduction to Botany* included Sarah Hoare's *Poem on the Pleasures and Advantages of Botanical Pursuits* in 1818.[16] Taken together, these texts represent the brief emergence of a hybrid genre of literature that presented science and poetry as mutually constructive yet not entirely compatible.

It was in this context of scientific, literary, and aesthetic experimentation that Elizabeth Kent published her *Flora Domestica* and *Sylvan Sketches*. In these collections, Kent treats common plants (in *Flora Domestica*) and trees (in *Sylvan Sketches*) in alphabetical order by common name, from Adonis to Zygophyllum and Acacia to Yew. Each entry begins with the common name of the plant, centered on the page in large font, followed by a secondary name, when available, in a slightly smaller font. On the next line, the plant's Latin name is given in small caps to the left, and the plant's classification according to the Linnaean sexual system is given in small caps to the right. A brief summary of the etymology of the plant's name follows in smaller font. The body of the entry provides, in no consistent order, information about the plant's defining characteristics, its origin and habitat, and proper care, as well as its appearances in mythology and literature. These texts, as their title pages proclaim, are illustrated not with lavish botanical drawings, but with "the works of the poets," and the works she excerpts range from classical to Cockney, with little concern for chronology or connections beyond the botanical.

The organization of the information of the page privileges a particular kind of reading in Kent's works. Darwin's *Botanic Garden* revels in the chaotic jumble of forms, as poetry, notes, and illustrations knock elbows on the page, and while the names of plants are visually emphasized within the text, the headings tend rather to interrupt the poem with Interludes than to indicate order. It is a poem that seems designed to disorient, yet it is also clearly intended to function as a single, disorienting whole (indeed, it is the unity itself that disorients). Smith's *Beachy Head* confines its notes to the end of the volume, and the text of the poem gives no indication that the reader might pause at any point to consult these notes. Although Smith herself was not involved in the final form of the published work, the structure urges readers to read the text as a whole, without interruption. Her *Conversations Introducing Poetry*, on the other hand, is organized into ten conversations, structured as if they were dialogue in a play; snippets of poetry are introduced by characters as they recite lines they have memorized. The book is structured to function pedagogically, allowing children to learn an ordered series of lessons alongside the characters in the book. Kent's works, however, are structured as reference materials, with key identifying information made visually prominent, presumably to aid a reader flipping through the

---

16   For a fuller treatment of these and other collections of botanical poetry by women authors, see Sam George, *Botany, Sexuality and Women's Writing, 1760–1830: From Modest Shoot to Forward Plant* (Manchester: Manchester University Press, 2007).

pages to find a particular entry. Kent provides a preface, but no unifying narrative. Rather, the reader might take up the book for a quick consultation about a particular plant, then set it back down. That is, the book is structured to facilitate engagement with a particular plant, to facilitate understanding of its ecological and literary habitat as constructed by Kent.

In Kent's works, science and poetry combine to illuminate a social dynamic, an affective relationship between humans and plants, and she pays particular attention to the human behaviors that might cause a plant to literally or metaphorically engage or withdraw. Both *Flora Domestica* and *Sylvan Sketches*, as Kent made explicit in the preface to each, were intended to serve as "introductions" in two senses: to introduce botanical knowledge to beginners in the field, and to serve as social introductions as between mutual friends. "[T]he intention of this volume," Kent writes in *Sylvan Sketches*, "is to give an unceremonious introduction of certain trees and shrubs to our readers, who are occasionally in the habit of meeting them without being acquainted, in many instances, even with their names."[17] She assumes that her readers have "met" these plants, but, "utterly ignorant of their wants and habits," have seen them "die one after the other, rather from attention ill-directed than from the want of it."[18] Like the plants of scientific experiment, Kent's are vulnerable, and sensitive—but they are vulnerable and sensitive in a very social sense, and this social vulnerability makes them frustratingly demanding companions, unable or unwilling to respond to or reciprocate our attentive care. The botanical knowledge conveyed in these pages is primarily a social knowledge, caught up in paying attention in a very particular way to beings that have "wants and habits" that they cannot communicate for themselves.

Kent's plants are responsive to human action (or inaction), and they also elicit human response. While Kent does not go so far as to imbue plants with consciousness, Kent portrays the intersubjective relationship between plants and humans as supporting and generating human self-awareness. In the preface to *Sylvan Sketches*, Kent writes,

> To attempt to enumerate the uses of the vegetable productions were to enter upon an endless theme indeed; as vain would it be to attempt to describe their beauties; but there is something beyond mere use, something beyond mere beauty, in their influence upon the human mind;—there is something in flowers and trees which excites our kindest sympathies, which soothes our keenest sorrows. (xv)

---

17   [Elizabeth Kent], *Sylvan Sketches; or, A Companion to the Park and the Shrubbery: With Illustrations from the Works of the Poets* (London: Taylor and Hessey, 1825), ix.
18   [Elizabeth Kent], *Flora Domestica, or the Portable Flower Garden; with Directions for the Treatment of Plants in Pots; and Illustrations from the Works of the Poets* (London: Taylor and Hessey, 1823), xiii.

Kent does not specify what that "something" is, or what the nature of those "kindest sympathies" might be when they are "excited" by a nonhuman subject. But their "influence upon the human mind" cannot be satisfactorily explained by either practical "use" or poetic "beauty." Kent calls attention to the interplay between scientific and poetic modes of knowledge at work in her project (and in other contemporary examples of this hybrid genre), while also calling attention to the limits of each mode, to the meaningful social encounters that we enter into with the vegetable other "beyond" our capacity to know that other.

The influence of plants on the human mind is particular *to* plants, as Kent makes clear when she compares human-animal relationships to human-plant relationships. "A man may indeed," she writes:

> love his horse or his dog, his monkey or his cat; may fondle a young tiger, or make a companion of a pet bear; but he will not lounge in a menagerie with his book, take a walk to Exeter Change to relieve his melancholy, or retire to his stable, or his dog-kennel, at twilight, to indulge in tranquil meditation. If he be weary, he will love to repose in the shade; if he be sad, he will love to wander in groves and woods; and, at the approach of sunset, he will doubly enjoy his book, his own thoughts, or the conversations of his friend, if he be seated under his favourite tree. (*Sylvan* xvi)

This passage has always struck me for its similarity to the Winnicottian holding environment which Nancy Yousef has extended to include the poetic frame of mind supported by the silent presence of the other.[19] In Yousef's analysis, the supporting other, who makes no demands on the poet's attention yet holds a place to which he may return, is by definition a conscious being who has withdrawn—or, rather, allowed the poet to withdraw without consequence. We cannot ascribe consciousness to the groves and woods Kent describes here, but their effect on the poetic mind mimics that of a consciousness that does not make demands on our attention.[20]

How to accord this withdrawn presence with the demanding plants of *Flora Domestica*, dying of "attention ill-directed"? What's taking shape here is a very social relationship in which the equal subjectivity of the beings involved cannot be assumed. Like the sensitive plants of scientific experiment, Kent's plants display vulnerability, perhaps even something approaching volition in their apparent "wants and needs." Yet Kent's plants cannot be understood through analogy to human or even animal consciousness. Rather, they participate in social exchanges that indicate a kind of consciousness that cannot be reduced to the knowable.

19   Nancy Yousef, "Romanticism, Psychoanalysis and the Interpretation of Silence," *European Romantic Review* 21, no. 5 (September 2010): 653–72.

20   At this point in the composition of this article, a cat jumped on my desk and sprawled across my notes and laptop in a helpful illustration of the difference between plants and animals.

2. Social Poets, Textual Ecosystems

Romanticism's social mind, as John Savarese demonstrated, has received increasing scholarly attention over the past two decades as what Gillian Russell and Clara Tuite describe as "Romanticism's traditional identification with the lone poet, withdrawn into productive introspection" has given way to scholarship celebrating the poetic school, the social network, the intersubjective experience, and the interaction.[21] Even the lone poet, as Kent's description in *Flora Domestica* illustrates, relies on the implicit support of a surrounding consciousness. Perhaps no school exemplified Romanticism's poetic sociability so much as the Cockney School centered around Leigh Hunt. As Jeffrey N. Cox argued in an early study of Romantic sociability, the Cockney poets, who at times included Keats, Shelley, Byron, and others, sought "to represent in verse the group and its life" by incorporating poetic dedications, poems written for Hunt's contests, and frequent invocations of other members of the group in an extensive intertextual network.[22] In many ways, Kent's botanical projects follow this pattern, reconstructing the social network of the Cockney School as a textual network. And by placing poetry from the Cockney School alongside classical and canonical poets including Milton, Ovid, Tasso, and Shakespeare, she elevates her community into an established poetic lineage outside the boundaries of time.

But consider for a moment Kent's actual position regarding the Cockney Circle. On the one hand, Kent often shared a home, even in gaol, with Leigh Hunt; she hosted social and intellectual gatherings, and helped establish the "poetic retreat from society" that allowed the circle to thrive.[23] But on the other hand, Kent was very much on the margins of the circle she had helped cultivate. Her fits of temper alienated even her closest friends, and until recently she was best known for "the anecdote that she threw herself into the pond at Hampstead one morning while Keats was waiting for his breakfast."[24] Even Hunt, who helped Kent gather the poetic specimens that illustrated her works, belittled her botanical work, writing in 1824 that "I think your little book," referring to her 1822 collection of children's stories, "beats your large one."[25] And his sonnet "To Miss K., Written on a Piece of Paper Which Happened to Be Headed with a Long List of Trees," literally erases her botanical work in favor of "two things richer far, / A verse and a staunch friend."[26] While Kent could represent

---

21   John Savarese, "Social Minds in Romanticism," *Literature Compass* 14, no. 2 (February 2017); Gillian Russell and Clara Tuite, eds, *Romantic Sociability: Social Networks and Literary Culture in Britain, 1770–1840* (Cambridge: Cambridge University Press, 2002), 4.

22   Jeffrey N. Cox, *Poetry and Politics in the Cockney School: Keats, Shelley, Hunt and Their Circle* (Cambridge: Cambridge University Press, 1998), 24.

23   Daisy Hay, *Young Romantics: The Shelleys, Byron, and Other Tangled Lives* (New York: Farrar, Straus and Giroux, 2010), 94.

24   Molly Tatchell, *Leigh Hunt and His Family in Hammersmith* (Hammersmith: Hammersmith Local History Group, 1969).

25   Leigh Hunt to Elizabeth Kent, 1 September 1824, *Leigh Hunt Letters*, University of Iowa Libraries, http://digital.lib.uiowa.edu/cdm/compoundobject/collection/leighhunt/id/71/rec/4.

26   Leigh Hunt, "To Miss K., Written on a Piece of Paper Which Happened to Be Headed with a Long List of Trees," *Foliage* (London: C. & J. Ollier, 1818).

in text the social circle of the Cockney School, it was difficult for her to participate in the actual social and literary life of the circle.

Kent's project is not just in conversation with the social constructs of the Cockney School; she is literally *constructing* that social network as a text. But also, and crucially, she is constructing that social network as a *botanical* text. While the Cockney poets incorporate intertextual elements and performative sociability into their poetic projects, Kent draws on the structure of botanical collections to frame her poetic anthologizing. Kent describes her botanical works as illustrated "from the works of the poets," and as Dahlia Porter recently argued, illustrations in botanical books at this time often functioned epistemically, "putting forward particular knowledge claims that may corroborate—but also extend, displace, or contradict—the import of the printed text."[27] Kent's "illustrations" function similarly, extending and complicating the claims asserted by a botanical work organized around Linnaean classifications. But this structure *also* complicates the claims that might be made through poetry or the interpretation of poetry. In a separate essay, Porter argues for an understanding of early nineteenth-century literary collections as borrowing from the scientific tradition of presenting botanical specimens.[28] Literary collections similarly gathered poetic "specimens" that had been ripped out of context (as one might remove a cut plant from its ecosystem) and presented as demonstrating the observable characteristics of a type. In this way, editors assembled literary anthologies that resemble scientific study. Although Porter does not mention her, Kent's work exemplifies the use of botanical collections to materially structure a poetic anthology. While Kent represents the social network of the Cockney School as a textual artifact, she also literally presents poetry in place of botanical specimens. Kent works on multiple registers of epistemic displacement to engage with and intervene in both poetic and scientific modes of knowledge construction.

Kent explicitly connects botanical collecting and the emerging form of the poetic anthology by 1825. At the time it was written, *Sylvan Sketches* would have had a double meaning: as Porter pointed out in another context, "sylvan" referred not only to trees, but also to "[c]lassical literary miscellanies."[29] Sylvae, according to the *Oxford English Dictionary*, were "'collections of poetical pieces, of various kinds, and on various subjects'" (*Science* 161). And in the updated preface to the 1825 second edition of *Flora Domestica*,[30] Kent compares her editorial project to the practice of flower-collecting, suggesting that what she chooses to include, and what she chooses to leave out, is less determined by a desire to collect the very best, than a desire to demonstrate

---

27   Dahlia Porter, "Epistemic Images and Vital Nature: Darwin's *Botanic Garden* as Image Text Book," *European Romantic Review* 29, no. 3 (June 2018): 296.

28   Dahlia Porter, "Specimen Poetics: Botany, Reanimation, and the Romantic Collection," *Representations* 139, no. 1 (Summer 2017): 60–94.

29   Porter, *Science, Form, and the Problem of Induction in British Romanticism*, 161.

30   Evidence of the alignment of the signature on the page indicates that an 1831 "New Edition" "Printed for Whittaker, Treacher, and Co," is most likely unsold stock from the 1825 second edition wrapped with a new title page and frontispiece.

the beauty found in a range of poetic endeavors. "There is an inspiration," she writes, "in the works of nature which gives a more than usual power even to talents of a common order, when treating of them; and although we take greater delight in the rose, the violet, or the lily, we also love to pluck from the hedge-side the hawthorn and the ragged-robin."[31] Kent supports this claim by quoting Wordsworth on "the inclination we have to gather wild flowers":

> We paused, one now,
> And now the other, to point out, perchance
> To pluck, some flower or water-weed, too fair
> Either to be divided from the place
> On which it grew, or to be left alone
> To its own beauty. (*Poems on the Naming of Places* xxxiv–xxxv)

While practical limitations of physical space prevent Kent from including all the "hedge-flowers of poetry" she might, Kent reminds us that both the practice of collecting flowers and the practice of collecting poetic excerpts involves an act of displacement that borders on violence as these specimens are removed from their ecosystems.

The imaginative home that a poet builds to surround the plants he observes, Kent suggests, forms an artificial ecosystem of textual associations. This ecosystem, she stresses, differs distinctly from the ecosystem that might be scientifically observed. "If flowers have so much beauty in common eyes," she writes:

> what must they be in the eye of a poet, which gives new charms to every object on which it gazes! A poet sees in a flower not only its form and colour, and the shadowing of its verdant foliage—his eye rests upon the dew-drop that trembles on the leaf; a gleam of sunshine darts across, and gives it the sparkling brilliancy of a diamond. He sees the bee hovering around, buzzing its joyous anticipation of the honey he shall draw from its very heart; and the delicate butterfly suspended as it were by magic from its silken petals. His imagination, too, brings around it a world of associations, adding beauty and interest to the object actually before his eye. (xxxvi)

In this passage, Kent articulates a distinction, which Richard M. Ness has noted in the poetry of John Clare, between the "decontextualized observation" of "*experiment*" and the "contextualized observation" of "*experience*."[32] Seeing a flower by its distinguishing (and classifying) characteristics of "form and colour" is not seeing the full environment of a particular and vivid moment in time that also includes dew, and sunshine, and the economy of bees. But, crucially, the poetic mode of observation is *also not* the experience of observation in the moment: the poetic observation extends beyond the plant and its context to "a world of associations" in the poet's own mind. As Ness says of Clare, Kent's passage "makes visible how aesthetics and science can be complicit in ecological harm. The scientist removes the insects [or plants] *from* their environment, while aesthetic conventions impose forms *onto* the environment" (17). But Kent is not arguing for resistance to either scientific or poetic decontextualization; rather, she is making use of both methods in order to perform an act of displacement herself as she plucks poetic specimens from their environment.

Kent uses the formal structure of botanical science to decontextualize, recontextualize, and *contain* the textual artifacts of a very social group of poets. While the practice of collecting botanical specimens disrupts the natural ecosystem, Kent acknowledges that her collection of *poetic* specimens disrupts and decontextualizes in order to imagine alternative poetic ecosystems, to create a new whole. She imposes a new structural environment onto the scraps of poetry she has gathered in a creative act that deserves to be recognized as an aesthetic intervention.

3. Senseless Weeds

The whole that Kent creates, she acknowledges, does not replicate the ecosystem that the poets represented would choose to inhabit. Yet that is exactly the point. In her preface to *Sylvan Sketches*, Kent explains her decision to bring together poetry by authors who would not voluntarily socialize: "Wordsworth speaks somewhere," she writes:

> of the tenderness of feeling excited by trees and flowers, a tenderness which, in the absence of those we love, is often wasted on the senseless weed. It is a conviction of this kindly influence of nature that has emboldened the writer to bring the most opposite parties together amid these woody scenes; not hesitating even to place Mr. Southey by the side of Lord Byron, without fear of the consequences, but rather indulging a faint hope that they may shake hands and be friends before they return to the irritating bustle of towns and cities. (xix)

The outpouring of "feeling" that might be seen as "wasted on the senseless weed," Kent reconceptualizes as integral to a friendliness that embraces fellow-feeling across difference. Her poetic reconfigurations productively redirect feeling, generating artificial affective networks that might, like poetry, have the tendency to *become* the truth they describe.

Many botanical writers of this period, particularly those who, like Kent, also wrote for and taught children, emphasized the value of careful observation leading to accurate identification.[33] And while Kent proposes to "introduce" plants to readers who might not even know their names, and provides careful descriptions that would allow readers to identify each plant, she also treats with *joy* the encounters made possible only through *mis*-identification. "Ariosto," she writes:

> although utterly ignorant of botanical science, took even an infantine pleasure in his little garden; and we are informed by his son, that after sowing a variety of seeds, he would watch eagerly for the springing of the plants, would cherish the first peep of vegetation, and having for many days watered and tended the young plant, discover at last that he had bestowed all this tenderness upon a weed; a weed, perhaps, which had choked the plant for which he had mistaken it. (*Flora* xiv–xv)

Rather than mourn the plants lost to Ariosto's failure to carefully observe and identify them, Kent celebrates his cultivation of the weed: "Who can read this anecdote of so great a man," she exults, "and not feel an additional interest in him! In how amiable a light it represents him!" (xv). In this charming anecdote, Ariosto's tenderness of feeling is affirmed through his *failure* to accurately observe the plants he nurtures. He cannot distinguish between the plants he *intends* to care for and the weeds that killed them—but the *care* persists beyond observation, classification, and intention. While this story is clearly delightful and entertaining and light-hearted, it also suggests a profound disconnect between what is *observable* and what is *ethical*.

Indeed, how poignant, given her struggles to find acceptance within her own social circle, is her description of the sensitive plant:

> Like human beings, they are more sensitive in proportion to the tenderness of their nursing; like them, by living hardily, they may be fitted to bear the common chances of life. In the plant, this nervous sensibility is encouraged for its singularity; it is pity there should not be the same reason for encouraging it in the human species. (*Flora* 247–8)

While many scientists and poets, in her time and ours, marveled at how the motion of the sensitive plant appeared to mimic the motion of human feeling, and used this similarity as the basis for analogical or allegorical links between plants, animals, and humans, Kent turns our attention to the ethical responsibility entailed in observing sensitivity in another. "Many persons have endeavoured to ascertain the cause of the sensibility of these plants," Kent continues:

---

33 Kent's collection of children's tales was recently identified by Leila Walker in "Elizabeth Kent's Lost *Tales*, Found," *North American Society for the Study of Romanticism* (conference presentation, Berkeley, CA, 11–14 August 2016).

but it has never yet been clearly explained. The degree varies in the different kinds: some will only contract their leaves on being touched; others will bend and recede, as it were courteously to acknowledge your approach; as that which is termed the Humble-plant. (248)

That the cause of the plant's sensitivity cannot be ascertained is not, for Kent, as ethically relevant as the social relation implied by its sensitivity. And this is important, because it suggests a subtle critique of our ability to develop social structures around observable interaction and intention. We cannot derive volition from the *appearance* of volition in the sensitive plant; nor can we expect the "senseless weed" to reciprocate the "tenderness of feeling" it might excite. We can observe how other beings respond, or fail to respond, to human contact, but this, ultimately, tells us more about what we are capable of recognizing as sensitivity than anything else.

It would be easy to read Elizabeth Kent's guides to the treatment of plants as metaphorical guides to the treatment of humans—and they are. They recall to us the joy of the accidental encounter, the importance of care for care's sake, the value in uniting, as Shelley put it, "all irreconcilable things" through acts of imagination.[34] But to read Kent's works as solely metaphorical would neglect how nimbly Kent negotiates the permeable boundary between poetry and science. While Darwin and Smith, as we have seen, engaged with both poetry and science in *The Botanic Garden* and *Beachy Head*, typographical and structural cues keep poetic and scientific modes of knowing distinct within each text. And although, as Porter has argued, the poetry does more than decorate the science, and the science does more than rationalize the poetry, it is also apparent that these authors carefully guard against confusion between the two. In Kent's works, however, science and poetry cohabitate easily within each entry, and this is important because it allows us to imagine bridging the gap between scientific and poetic ways of knowing.

While the gap between science and poetry is made literally, visibly apparent in the physical structure of *The Botanic Garden* and *Beachy Head*, no such structural cues call attention to a knowledge gap in *Flora Domestica* and *Sylvan Sketches*. Instead, Kent moves quickly between scientific observation, poetic illustration, and her own act of interpretation mediating between the two. In the entry on the *Mimosa*, for example, she begins by providing instructions for the proper care of the plant before comparing its care to the proper care of humans, then turns back to the practical matter of proper potting and watering, summarizes the scientific failure to explain the plant's movements, excerpts relevant selections from two poems, and finally concludes by describing the plant's natural habitat. Natural segues do not always connect this jumble of associations. Rather, poetry and potting are treated as equally important to the plant's "biography" and proper care. But there remains a gap between poetic

34   Percy Bysshe Shelley, "A Defence of Poetry," in *Percy Bysshe Shelley: The Major Works*, ed. Zachary Leader and Michael O'Neill (Oxford: Oxford University Press, 2003), 698.

and scientific modes of knowing, which Kent makes clear in a later discussion of the sensitive plant.

In the preface to *Sylvan Sketches*, Kent returns to the poetic treatment of the *Mimosa*, in this case highlighting a Matthew Prior poem in which Solomon asks the learned:

> Whence does it happen that the plant which well
> We name the sensitive, should move and feel?
> Whence know her leaves to answer her command,
> And with quick horror fly the approaching hand?

Kent interprets:

> The learned could not answer these inquiries; neither could they have explained why certain plants are so choice in the selection of their friends, that they will turn from such as do not please them. We cannot suppose this to be without reason: plants are too amiable to indulge in causeless antipathies. (xxxii)

In this passage, Kent fills the gap in scientific understanding of the sensitive plant's motions with a poetic treatment of that gap; she allows poetry to reveal the work that science is unable to do, enabling her to intuit, in the interpretive space that opens up between science and poetry, the existence of a consciousness whose existence is beyond the bounds of our understanding. Kent's works draw on the botanical practice of scientific observation in order to expose the limits of *both* scientific and poetic observation, forcing readers to consider the value of consciousnesses (and sensitivities) we cannot observe. She calls our attention to the questions neither science nor poetry can *ask*, to the gap between observable reality and observation and interpretation.

At the heart of Kent's observations on the sensitive plant is the firm belief that plants must be understandable, even if they are not understandable *to us*. Kent presents plants as beings who might place demands on our attention, or release us from the obligation of attention; beings who cannot be fully understood, but nonetheless share intersubjective experiences. She allows them to remain strange even in their familiarity, even as they become more familiar through Kent's introductions. Even with the most careful attention to its "wants and habits," the sensitive plant may still turn away, or not. We are inclined to interpret this turning away as a response *to us*, to the care or harm we mete out, in experiential or experimental environments. But that would be "attention ill-directed."

There's violence in the assumption that if we pay proper attention to another being, it will, or must, *respond*. In the quest to conceive of another being's consciousness as interpretable by us, we perhaps make our investigations into its consciousness (or lack thereof) really *about* us. But in her descriptions of sensitive plants and senseless weeds, Kent leaves intact the other's right to love us or ignore us for no reason that we can perceive.

As the philosopher Michael Marder has recently argued, "the absolute familiarity of plants coincides with their sheer strangeness." "More often than not," he writes, "we overlook trees, bushes, shrubs, and flowers in our everyday dealings, to the extent that these plants form the inconspicuous backdrop of our lives."[35] Like the landscapes that support the mental wanderings of a poet allowed to withdraw, Marder's inconspicuous plants blur into an undifferentiated mass of green. "How," Marder asks, "is it possible for us to encounter plants? And how can we maintain and nurture, without fetishizing it, their otherness in the course of this encounter?" Encounters that would contain plants within systems of classification, that focus on naming a plant and identifying it with a particular species, he persuasively argues, obscure the plant itself in a series of abstractions and generalizations. Instead, he suggests, "the idea is to allow plants to flourish on the edge or at the limit of phenomenality, of visibility, and, in some sense, of 'the world.'" As Kent puts it, we encounter plants "beyond" our ability to explain.

While Kent's works allow readers to identify plants with their type, the artificiality of such naming becomes clear as scientific and literary systems are applied simultaneously; science, like literature, abstracts the real. Yet these abstractions allow us to acknowledge an encounter with a different mode of being. Kent facilitates encounters with plants that disrupt the "green wall" and allow us to see individual plants by "introducing" her readers to them, their care, and their poetic treatment.[36] Like the killer plants and "strange orchids" that would populate Victorian literature years later, Kent's plants have a kind of "narrative agency" that, as Elizabeth Chang has argued, "radically [alter] notions about sentience, mobility, reproduction, and representation—not least by blurring distinctions between character and setting."[37] The structure of Kent's works inclines toward such blurring, as Kent constructs a hybrid literary form in which the "holding" environment the natural landscape provides the poet is reconstituted in text as the frame "holding" the poetic results.

---

35   Michael Marder, *Plant Thinking: A Philosophy of Vegetal Life* (New York: Columbia University Press, 2013), 3.

36   Professional kitten rescuer Hannah Shaw speaks eloquently of her experience learning to "see" plants: "I remember when I used to go into the forest for a hike, I would just see a green wall. Sure, I understood that there were lots of plants, but I didn't know much about them. They were a group— 'plants'—and that group was a green wall. As I developed an interest in plants, the green wall began to change. I got to know the tulip poplars, which were often friends to morels after a good rain. I started to notice the lichens that would cling to the bark of fallen trees, and I could even identify a few—'hey wait a minute, I know you! You're usnea.' The more time I spent in nature, the more the green wall disappeared and the green space was alive with individuals" (Instagram post, 27 May 2019, https://www.instagram.com/p/Bx-NKSfJ18X/).

37   Elizabeth Chang, "Killer Plants of the Late Nineteenth Century," in *Strange Science: Investigating the Limits of Knowledge in the Victorian Age*, ed. Lara Karpenko and Shalyn Claggett (Ann Arbor: University of Michigan Press, 2016), 83.

In this way, she constructs an intertextual sociality in which plants participate in the same ecosystem of thought as the Cockney Poets themselves.

And yet, despite Kent's introductions, and despite their vital presence within a social system, these plants remain fundamentally *strange*. Marder contemplates at length the concept of "vegetal indifference"—that is, a plant's fundamental indifference to itself (or "its 'self'") as a unified being (132). Plant thinking, in this sense, can never be understood through analogy to human or even animal thinking, because the sense of the self doing the thinking is so radically different. We lose sight of this difference in the poetic use of plants as symbols, allegories, and metaphors for the human condition, rather than for themselves. Kent, by cataloging these poetic uses within the structure of botanical introductions, centers the *relationship* between human and plant—she never allows us to lose sight of the *plant itself* in the imposed environments of poetic imagination or scientific classification. The structure of her texts, which encourages readers to consult the book as they encounter specific plants in nature or poetry, asserts the primacy of a personal relationship, an encounter with an other being that cannot adequately be described in any genre of human thought. Like Marder, Kent refuses to "assert an unconditional right of admission into the vegetal world, which is the world *of* and *for* plants, accessible to them" (8–9). Even with a proper introduction, plants may still withdraw from us, or not; may thrive, or not; may love us in ways we are incapable of understanding. Our ethical responsibility is to pay attention without the expectation of full comprehension.

4. Coda

As I write this article, in 2019, I sit in an office surrounded by plants in various stages of propagation: a rubber tree rescued from the curb when a neighbor died without relatives; two sprawling pothos clipped from colleagues' plants; three paperwhites that do not seem inclined to flower; six tiny clippings from a jade plant given to me by a dear friend sixteen years ago. The jade plant once flourished, but my cat ate it and then urinated on it seven years ago; two cuttings from that first disaster managed to survive before both began, inexplicably, to rot from the roots last month. The six tiny cuttings, no more than a leaf or two each, are all that now survive. I still think of all these plants as the original and call them each by the same name; they defy distinction between individuality and plurality. I do hope that they reward my efforts by thriving.

While I have always loved plants, it must be said that my current fascination is part of a larger trend. If "put a bird on it" was the dominant aesthetic of 2011, the corresponding catchphrase for 2019 must surely be "put a plant on it." In the past two years, it seems every magazine that runs think-pieces has run at least one think-piece on why Millennials love plants. (I must clarify that, despite my interest in plants, I am not myself a Millennial.) The generational psychology behind this trend has been explained in various ways that all reflect on this particular historic moment: it's compensation for the delay in parenthood or home ownership forced by strained economic conditions;[38] it's a reaction to fears about climate change;[39] it's an expression of self-care;[40] it's for Instagram.[41] These explanations do exactly what explanations of any trends attributed to Millennials do: homogenize and infantilize a diverse generation that is rapidly entering middle age, while reducing human encounters to the logic of capitalism. And as cultural critic Kate Wagner put it in a think-piece responding to these think-pieces, "a general rule of capitalism throughout history is: what's good for business is usually bad for living things."[42]

The logic of capitalism necessitates the commodification the encounter with the plant; it transforms living plants into things that can be categorized with a hashtag and monetized at scale. To resist this, Wagner argues in language strikingly similar to Kent's, we must recognize that "[t]he true joy of houseplant ownership comes via observation and attention." We must attune ourselves to plants *as* plants, animate in their own slow way, conscious as only plants can be conscious. We must attend to their differences in order to see them as similarly valuable. "We see plants as inanimate objects," Wagner writes,

> because they change and react to their environment on a much longer timescale than animals. We have the mistaken idea that plants do not respond to human love in the same way that animals do, that plants cannot feel in the traditional sense. No, a houseplant isn't the same thing as a dog, but it is closer to a dog than it is to an image of a dog.

And we have an ethical responsibility to *care* for houseplants *because* they are plants. "This caring isn't an inconvenience of houseplants," Wagner stresses, "it is the very *reason for having them*." This care manifests in actions—maintaining a comfortable environment, attending to the plant's wants and needs, talking to the plant and washing its leaves—but it also manifests in a desire to *know* the plants. In the conclusion to her article, Wagner declares, "I'm done with books about which pots look good with African Violets or how to pair plants with vintage cameras. Tell me what these plants *are*, where they come from, why they look and behave the way they do."

38   Lisa Boone, "They Don't Own Homes. They Don't Have Kids. Why Millennials Are Plant Addicts," 24 July 2018, https://www.latimes.com/home/la-hm-millennials-plant-parents-20180724-story.html.
39   Jia Tolentino, "The Leafy Love Affair Between Millennials and Houseplants," *The New Yorker*, 18 April 2019, https://www.newyorker.com/culture/culture-desk/the-leafy-love-affair-between-millennials-and-our-houseplants.
40   Hillary Hoffower, "Millennials Really Love Plants," *Business Insider*, 12 April 2019.
41   Matthew Boyle, "The One Thing Millennials Haven't Killed Is Houseplants," *Bloomberg*, 11 April 2019, https://www.bloomberg.com/news/features/2019-04-11/the-one-thing-millennials-haven-t-killed-is-houseplants.
42   Kate Wagner, "Plant Parenthood," *The Baffler*, 9 July 2019, https://thebaffler.com/kate-takes/plant-parenthood-wagner.

Perhaps it is time once again to attend to Elizabeth Kent, not only as a figure in the history of literature and science, but as an author who might help us more purposefully observe our communities that include both human and nonhuman actors. Who better to answer (or gently refuse to answer) Wagner's questions: "Why do calatheas have so many variations in their leaf patterns? Why do some plants fold up at night? How did these plants relate to other species in their native habitats? Who discovered them and classified them? How have they been used culturally?" Science can answer some of these questions, poetry others. Both forms of knowledge allow us to encounter plants in the gap between them, as strangely familiar and worthy, in their strangeness, of our care.

Acknowledgements

This article was made possible in part by the generous award of a Directors' Scholarship to Rare Book School. An early version of this work was presented at the *MLA Annual Convention* on the "Romanticism and Embodied Cognition" panel. My thanks to Richard Sha for convening the panel, to Jonathan Kramnick for his illuminating response, and to Kate Singer and her students at Mt. Holyoke College for their provocative questions.

Important Notice

Liverpool University Press is pleased to announce the migration of all journals to a new bespoke online platform, hosted by Cloud Publish.

www.liverpooluniversitypress.co.uk/journals

Our previous website currently has redirects in place and your access to subscribed journals will not be interrupted.

If you have any questions about the migration please contact Clare Hooper, Head of Journals, at clare.hooper@liverpool.ac.uk.

https://doi.org/10.3828/eir.2020.27.2.4

Precarious Correspondence in
The Woman of Colour

Deven M. Parker
Queen Mary University of London

The anonymous 1808 novel, *The Woman of Colour,* one of the few works of the Romantic period to prominently feature a woman of mixed-race African descent, begins *in medias res*—not just because we happen upon Olivia Fairfield, our heroine, on her journey from Jamaica to England to meet the cousin whom she must marry—but also because her correspondence begins in the middle of the Atlantic Ocean, a strange reversal of the middle passage that her enslaved African mother experienced decades earlier.[1] Writing to her former governess, Mrs. Milbanke, Olivia reels as she is forced to leave her home in order to meet the demands of her dead father's will, "launched on a new world ... to tempt the untried deep and untried friends."[2] Her experience of literal and metaphorical groundlessness as she is carried across the sea by circumstances beyond her control is also reflected in the scene of writing: the date and place at the top of her letter are simply given as "at Sea, on board the **.**. 180—" (53). This lack of date and clear sense of places continues for the duration of the novel, with Olivia beginning her letters with "in continuation" even as she moves between different locations in England. We get relatively little sense of how long her journey across the sea takes, or even how much time separates the events that transpire once she settles in England. Formally, the novel breaks with the epistolary novel tradition of a series of discrete letters as it is divided into "packets"— referring, as Broadview editor Lyndon Dominique notes, both to a "collection of letters but also the mailboats used to carry them to Jamaica" (53)—that contain dozens of individual letters that run together given their lack of dates. Reflecting the material realities of transatlantic correspondence, the novel's irregular form mirrors its heroine's state of precarity.

Readings of *The Woman of Colour* rightly focus on how Olivia navigates English society as a mixed-race woman—how, as the illegitimate daughter of a white plantation owner and an enslaved African woman, she manages to expose the

---

1   Jennifer DeVere Brody also makes this comparison in *Impossible Purities: Blackness, Femininity, and Victorian Culture* (Durham and London: Duke University Press, 1998), 23. In addition, she argues that Olivia Fairfield's body is itself "a material reminder (and remainder) of ... circum-Atlantic encounters" (15).

2   Anonymous, *The Woman of Colour*, ed. Lyndon J. Dominique (1808; Peterborough: Broadview Press, 2007), 53.

racism and hypocrisy of white England, advance an abolitionist agenda, and, at the novel's conclusion, secure her economic independence and return home to Jamaica. This ending, where Olivia declares herself a metaphorical widow, rejects an offer of marriage, regains her inheritance, and returns to Jamaica to educate the enslaved, has provoked a number of interpretations, all of which seem to agree that Olivia achieves something like autonomy or independence, successfully resisting the demands of her dead father's will and escaping white English society. For example, Brigette Fielder's analysis of Olivia's relationship with her black servant and companion, Dido, reveals how, in the women's departure for Jamaica, "Olivia ultimately rejects the social reproduction of Englishness, whiteness, and empire, and embraces kinship with the African diaspora of the colonies."[3] Melissa Adams-Campbell, too, emphasizes the Olivia's successful attempt at resistance, arguing that the heroine's "pathbreaking conclusion creates a new pattern of domesticity ... . She makes a place for herself and for the Caribbean within the dominant ideology of domesticity."[4]

This essay revisits the questions these readings have brought to light—whether, by the book's end, Olivia is able to take control of her body and situation in spite of the racism that works against her—by approaching them from the perspective of the novel's epistolary form, an aspect of the work that has received little attention. Specifically, I examine an important historical and material context evoked in the novel that, I claim, mediates its form and narrative: Britain's international packet boat network. Like the other communication networks that proliferated at the time, the packet trade's expansion in the Romantic period came as a result of the ongoing war with France. As a branch of the Post Office, it, like England's domestic mail service, served as a de-facto branch of the state military as it was used to convey military intelligence and crack down on foreign espionage during the Napoleonic wars. Yet, unlike the mail and the other state-sponsored telecommunication networks that arose in this period, the packet network actually became a less secure, more precarious mode of communication and trade during this period thanks to its elevated military importance. As crucial conveyors of Britain's strategic intelligence, packet boats were targeted by French privateers, who, at the direction of Napoleon himself, frequently captured them. Given the importance of their cargo, captains of packet boats were instructed to toss mail overboard rather than allow it to be seized by the French.

3   "The Woman of Colour and Black Atlantic Movement," in Women's Narratives of the Early Americas and the Formation of Empire, ed. Mary Balkun and Susan Imbarrato (New York and London: Palgrave, 2016), 183.

4   Melissa M. Adams-Campbell, New World Courtships: Transatlantic Alternatives to Companionate Marriage (Hanover: Dartmouth College Press, 2015), 98. In "Models of Morality: The Bildungsroman and the Social Reform in The Female American and The Woman of Colour" (Women's Studies 45, no. 7 [2016]: 613–23), Victoria Barnett-Woods also claims that Olivia liberates herself by the novel's ending (622). See also Lyndon J. Dominique's critique in Imoinda's Shade: Marriage and the African Woman in Eighteenth-Century British Literature, 1757–1808 (Columbus: The Ohio State University Press, 2012), which I treat in part two of this essay.

Others have rightly positioned *The Woman of Colour* in the context of the 1807 Slave Trade Act as well as ongoing debates about abolition, but I think that, in addition to this crucial context, the Napoleonic packet network serves as an additional, perhaps less obvious context that, when brought to light, also works as a lens through which the novel develops its critique of slavery, racism, and empire. Put simply, the novel uses one structure—its own packet form—to criticize another. I want to consider the indelible marks that the precarious, politicized packet network had on the individual packets of letters that circulated within it, and how the expansion and militarization of the packet trade illuminates *The Woman of Colour*'s unique transatlantic epistolary form. I argue that, read within this context, Olivia's correspondence contributes to the novel's broader preoccupation with its protagonist's unstable identity, conflating her body with packets that circulate in an increasingly unstable wartime network. This lack of control on the part of the heroine is also highlighted by the fact that her letters are subjected to the heavy hand of an editor. In contrast to others' optimistic readings of the ending, my reading suggests that the novel's conclusion actually casts doubt on Olivia's ability to acquire agency or independence as a woman of color and instead offers a pessimistic critique of England's entwined systems of racism and misogyny. *The Woman of Colour* deploys state-controlled media not as a means of harnessing institutional power in a bid for feminist agency, but rather as a way of revealing the impossibility for women of color to take control of their lives within such structures.

1. "Sea-worthy sentiments": Packet Networks in the Early Ninteenth Century

Off the coast of Barbados on the morning of 1 October 1807—about a year before *The Woman of Colour* saw print—an English packet boat, the *Windsor Castle*, raised the alarm that a French privateer, the *Jeune Richard*, was preparing to overtake them. Unable to outrun the enemy vessel, the packet's captain, William Rogers, instructed his small crew of twenty-eight to secure anti-boarding nets and prepare to return cannon fire. By some miracle, the French crew of ninety-two were unable to board and, receiving significant damage from the small packet, surrendered their ship to Rogers and his five surviving crewmen. Rogers boarded the privateer, killed her captain, and hoisted English colors, claiming the ship for his nation in what was truly a remarkable outcome for the captain and crew of a small mail delivery vessel. To commemorate the victory and Rogers—who quickly became a national hero after news of the event made the rounds in London's newspapers—Samuel Drummond painted the scene in a work exhibited at the Royal Academy in 1808, and which currently is on display at the National Maritime Museum in Greenwich [FIGURE 1]. In the painting, Rogers stands aboard the deck of the *Jeune Richard*, preparing to shoot the privateer's boatswain, surrounded at all sides by the French crew, at least three of whom are black. As Megan Lowena Oldcorn observes, Rogers, "surrounded by a light that seems to emanate from him, [he] is unperturbed by the sword that is about to be brought down upon his head, or by the dead body his enemy stands on."[5] The painting emphasizes his bravery and suggesting divine favor even as the odds outweigh him. Striking a heroic posture, he emerges amidst the chaos of the skirmish to prevail over the enemy intent on stealing the packet boat. Given that his job, to put it simply, was to deliver the mail, it is perhaps surprising that Rogers received an artistic depiction on par with the heroes of Waterloo and Trafalgar.

While Rogers's capture of the *Jeune Richard* was by no means business as usual for the crew of a packet boat—vessels built to outrun rather than fight the enemy—I open with this scene because Rogers's defense of the packet, coupled with his deification in Drummond's painting, illustrates both the supreme importance of the packet trade to the Admiralty and the dangers it faced in the early nineteenth century. Oldcorn has argued that during the Napoleonic Wars "the Packet ship changed from being a carrier of news and mail to a fully-fledged military vessel," an "unofficial intelligence body" even though it was not considered an official branch of the Royal Navy (40–2). Like the Post Office in England, it served as an extension of the Home Office, charged not just with ensuring the safe circulation of important government correspondence but also with surveilling international waters in order to provide early reports of French military action, especially in West Indian waters where both France and Britain maintained slave colonies. We might interpret Richards's defense of his ship, then, as promoting the interests of Britain's national security rather than simply personal correspondence between England and Barbados.

The first packet routes between England and the Caribbean were established as early as 1689 and were based in Falmouth, a town on the coast of Cornwall in Southwest England. As a branch of the Post Office, the packet network transported and delivered mail overseas before connecting with the mainland mail routes. The number of packet routes steadily increased as the eighteenth century drew to a close, with thirty-nine in operation by the time *The Woman of Colour* was published in 1808. The service was in such high demand by this time that temporary ships had to be drafted (Oldcorn 39). Although the service did not come under the direct control of the Admiralty until 1823, the network became increasingly militarized in conjunction with the rest of the Post Office. Naval historian Arthur Norway points to 1793 as the year that the British military took its first real interest in using the network to advance its interests, cracking down on the rampant smuggling that had previously plagued the service. Seizing the packet trade away from the control of private merchants, who had earlier dictated its movements and operations, the Royal Navy put into place several polices that point to its de-facto control of the network when war with France broke out. For example, existing packet crewmembers at Falmouth were officially exempted from impressment, suggesting that the Admiralty believed they were more or less already part of the Navy or that they had fulfilled an important role (Oldcorn 15). Again, if seized by the enemy, packet crew were

FIGURE 1: Samuel Drummond, *Captain William Rogers capturing the* Jeune Richard, *1 October 1807* (1808), National Maritime Museum, Greenwich Hospital Collection. My thanks to the Royal Museums Greenwich Picture Library for permission to reprint this image.

given top priority in terms of exchange and rescue, even above regular members of the Navy. In January 1799, Francis Freeling, the Secretary General of the Post Office, sent a request to the Lords of the Admiralty for the exchange and release of sixty-one capture packet crewmembers, underscoring their importance to the ongoing war effort.

The packets' importance was especially heightened during the Napoleonic wars, when Napoleon initiated a blockade of Europe and banned commercial shipping between England and the continent. Only packets were allowed to travel into hostile waters, but that did not stop French privateers from trying to seize their cargo. Moreover, between 1803 and 1815, packets functioned as part of the Post Office's little-known "Secret Office," a branch with the intended purpose of intercepting enemy mail, and which installed counter-intelligence measures to protect English mail from being seized (Oldcorn 56). Interestingly, the primary medium of surveillance that packets employed were crewmembers' personal journals and writings, in which they recorded daily events that sometimes included the movements of enemy ships. Packets also communicated with each other via flag signals. Important extracts of these journals were delivered to the Postmaster General and the Admiralty upon a ship's arrival in Falmouth. Under the guise of providing a postal service, packets effectively spied on foreign communications.

All of that said, even as the Packet Service expanded under the direction of the Admiralty, its ships and their cargo remained extremely vulnerable to enemy attacks and destruction. In this case, heightened military importance actually threatened the network's security rather than improving it. This was in part because of the Royal Navy's preferred strategy of having packets try to outrun privateers rather than engage them in conflict. The lightweight ships were outfitted with relatively few guns so that they could more easily outstrip the pursuit of military vessels, despite the fervent requests of West Indian merchants who worried for the security of the goods they shipped on them. Instructions to crew members in the case of an attack included the following: "You must run where you can. You must fight when you can no longer run, and when you can fight no more you must sink the mails before you strike."[6] Indeed, all packet boats were equipped with special nets that allowed the crew to sling bundles of mail over the side of the boat in anticipation of being boarded. The defensive practice of sinking the mail indicates its military importance but also highlights mail's material fragility aboard packets. One's correspondence with a loved one halfway across the world might end up alongside secret military papers and become collateral damage if the more important document needed to be destroyed as a security precaution. In the Admiralty's mind, it was a necessary sacrifice; between 1793 and 1815, the enemy successfully seized nineteen English packets thanks in part to American privateers recruited by the French. Many of these operated with the intended purpose of intercepting packets, which were considered a prize even more valuable than merchant ships. Things were extremely dangerous for mail transported through the Caribbean, "where the French gained lurking places in every creek of the

---

6   Arthur H. Norway, *History of the Post-office Packet Service Between the Years 1793–1815. Compiled from Records, Chiefly Official* (London: Macmillan and Co., 1895), 38.

Spanish islands, and were enabled to lie in ambush for British commerce at numberless points where our ships were used to think themselves in safety" (Norway 69). In 1806, three consecutive packets bound for England from Jamaica and Barbados were seized, meaning that even merchants who sent their letters in triplicate as an added security measure were in trouble. Around this time, Henry Dundas, Secretary of State for the English colonies, sent duplicate and triplicate copies of his dispatches via merchant vessels "which appear to have a better chance of safe arrival than the regular Packets" (91). Like Dundas, many in this period of severe conflict began to view packets as "too unreliable and transient" (Oldcorn 43). Even civilians who travelled aboard packets as passengers—a relatively common practice—were brought into the line of fire: a French attack on a boat in Jamaica's Cumberland Harbor saw the death of one such person along with the loss of the mail (Norway 45). Ships that arrived safely in Falmouth following a transatlantic journey emerged "battered, blackened and damaged, with hulls, spars, and sails shattered, and with ensigns half-masted in honour of the dead" (Oldcorn 45). Personal mail that survived the journey unscathed was then subject to the Post Office's homeland security measures, carefully examined, and sorted before being allowed to progress to its destination.

The instability of the packet network left its mark on the mail that circulated within it, whether it was thrown overboard, seized by privateers, or charred and battered by the time it arrived in Falmouth. Writing to a correspondent in Australia in his essay "Distant Correspondents," Charles Lamb reflects at length on the impact of the packet trade on both the material form of the letter and the sentiments it contains, all but arguing that his awareness of its dangerous journey inhibits his ability to express himself within the medium. For Lamb, the networks that enable long distance correspondence also depersonalize it, transforming the letter's form and content over the course of its circulation:

> It is difficult to conceive how a scrawl of mine should ever stretch across [the ocean]. It is a sort of presumption to expect that one's thoughts should live so far [...]. [C]onceive the sentiment boarded up, freighted, entered at the Custom House [...] hoisted into a ship. Conceive it pawed about and handled between rude jests of tarpaulin ruffians—a thing of its delicate texture—the salt bilge wetting it till it became as vapid as a damaged lustring [...] till at length it arrives at its destination, tired out and jaded, from a brisk sensation, into a feature of silly pride or tawdry senseless affectation.[7]

What interests me here are the material changes the letter undergoes over the course of its journey from sender to receiver as it moves through the packet network.

---

7   Charles Lamb, *Elia. Essays Which Have Appeared under that Signature in the London Magazine* (London: Printed for Taylor and Hessey, Fleet Street, 1823), 238–40.

Beginning simply as a "scrawl," its sentimental character only shines through once it is set against the backdrop of the Custom House: the official procedures it must undergo work to highlight its sentimental quality by way of contrast. The range of bodies and objects with which it comes into contact over the course of its journey likewise serve to emphasize its delicacy because of how easily they damage it, as if it were a fragile, silken fabric. When it finally arrives at its destination, the medium has been so altered that what once read as delicate, personal sentiments now read as "silly" and "tawdry," the object bearing physical reminders of the great distance it traveled. The methods of its conveyance transform the appearance of the thing in question and therefore its message. Indeed, letters coming out of London also bore this connection to an even greater extent as they came into contact with wet newspapers being transported on the same mail coach. The ink stains left on them served as reminders of their participation in a larger network of print circulation and government-regulated communication. Lamb reminds us of the materiality of documents circulating within these politically-charged networks and of the interconnections between different forms of communication.

One of the most important media of communication during this period, particularly in regard to the circulation of military information, the Packet Network nonetheless emerged as an increasingly unstable, unreliable mode of correspondence, albeit the only option one had if one wanted to communicate overseas. Both politically inflected and precarious, the network to which correspondents entrusted their personal mail had the potential to transform those letters and objects and, as in Lamb's experience, infiltrate their contents. The packet network's schedule and rhythms—the dates of departing boats were announced in the papers, providing deadlines for letter writers—often dictated the form and scope of a letter, as, for example, when John Keats, writing to his brother in America, broke off only when a ship was about to depart for Philadelphia, which was infrequent.[8] In contrast other modes of communication that became increasingly secure and regular over the course of the century, such as the domestic Post, communicating through the Packet Network involved risking not just the privacy of one's letters but also their physical safety.

2. "a mere *state machine*": Olivia Fairfield's Packets

The Woman of Colour opens with its heroine embarking on a voyage from Jamaica to England that, given the violence and turmoil that characterized transatlantic passages at the height of the Napoleonic wars, was more dangerous than it might at first appear to readers. Not only must Olivia Fairfield travel to a foreign country to meet the demands of her father's will—to marry her cousin, Augustus, in order to receive her

---

8   See, for example, Keats's letter to his brother George of 31 October 1818, when he breaks off because "there will not be a Philadelphia Ship for these six weeks" (405). "To George and Georgiana Keats, 14–31 October 1819," in *The Letters of John Keats, 1814–1821*, ed. Hyder Edwards Rollins (Cambridge, M.A.: Harvard University Press, 1958). My thanks to Brian Rejack for tracking down this reference.

fortune—she must also "tempt the untried deep" (53), setting out on a voyage at the height of a war that saw numerous civilian casualties. Her "packets"—the bundles of letters she sends to her former governess back in Jamaica—are, like other mail sent across the water at this time, in danger of being stolen or destroyed on their journey, vulnerable objects that mirror Olivia's bodily vulnerability as she is thrust into circumstances beyond her control. While I agree with Lyndon Dominique's reading that the novel's epistolary form "allows Olivia to control the way she represents her undeniably Negroid body" (*Imoinda's Shade* 248) in English society, I view any autonomy she gains through self-representation as ultimately undercut by the precarity of the novel's packet context. The content of her letters is, as in the novels of so many others during this period, mediated by the technology of the communication medium through which they travel. The novel formally enacts this precarious mediation through its editorial ruptures. Reading these breaks alongside moments in the narrative proper in which Olivia is continually acted upon by others, I think the novel uses her packets to underscore her helplessness and lack of agency, conflating them with her physical body. Rather than concluding with a hopeful ending in which its heroine triumphantly returns to Jamaica as economically independent, the novel's pattern of formal and narrative precarity in the form of packets casts doubt on her ability to achieve this goal and instead offers a pessimistic view of her future as a mixed-race subject unable to move freely within the transatlantic spaces of the early nineteenth century.

It is worth recounting the novel's plot since it only recently joined the Romantic canon after being understudied for more than two centuries.[9] We learn that Olivia is the mixed-race daughter of a white plantation owner and his black slave. Her father, who has recently died, included a clause in his will that Olivia may only receive her large inheritance if she goes to England to marry her white cousin, Augustus. Otherwise, Mr. Fairfield's fortune will pass to Augustus's brother and his wife, Letitia Merton, with Olivia kept as their ward. On her voyage to England, Olivia is accompanied by her black servant, Dido, and befriends a Mrs. Honeywood and her son, a white man born in Jamaica. Upon arriving in England, Olivia experiences intense racism from most around her but particularly from Letitia Merton, who unsuccessfully attempts to prejudice Augustus against Olivia. Despite hints that Augustus's heart lies elsewhere, he eventually decides to marry Olivia, and the newlyweds settle in a large countryside home, where Olivia encounters more racism at the hands of her new neighbors. However, after a few months of relative happiness, Olivia learns that Augustus was previously married, and that the wife he had presumed dead, Angelina, has suddenly returned to him with their child in tow. We learn that Angelina's disappearance and sudden reappearance were orchestrated by Letitia Merton, whom Augustus had jilted in his youth. His reunion with Angelina

---

9   The novel reentered the canon thanks to the enormous editorial labor of Lyndon Dominique. His Broadview Press edition remains the only version in print.

means that he and Olivia were never legally married, putting Olivia and her fortune in Letitia's control. Distraught, Olivia retreats with Dido to a cottage on the border of Wales, where Honeywood eventually finds her and proposes. In a surprising turn of event for a novel seemingly in the genre of a sentimental narrative controlled by the marriage plot, Olivia refuses him and declares herself a widow; she then decides to return to Jamaica to work as a teacher of the enslaved.

From the beginning of her journey, Olivia's future is almost entirely out of her hands. Although she tries to rationalize the demands of her father's will—that she marry his nephew who resides in England in order to receive her fortune, or else become the ward of the nephew's older brother and wife—by speculating that his "generous intention" was to "secure his child a proper protector in a husband" (55) and where, he imagined, she would experience less cruelty as a woman of color, Dominique and other readers have rightly observed that the effect of such a will is to ensure that Mr. Fairfield's legacy—his descendants and the recipients of his wealth—will be white.[10] Furthermore, we learn that Augustus, Olivia's betrothed, is "the image" (59) of Mr. Fairfield himself, a revelation, according to Dominique, "clearly evoking a crime of incest only once removed from the plantation" (27). Even though Olivia tries to understand the rationale for her father's decision, she admits to a companion on the ship, Mrs. Honeywood,

> I frequently think, that I can talk as coolly, and with as little *mauvaise honte* of this intended alliance as if I were a mere *state machine!*— conveyed over the water at the instigation of political contrivance; yet believe me, my dear madam, I have a sense of my sex's more exclusive feeling delicacy. My heart revolts, it shrinks within me nearer to the scene of my trial; and the anxiety with which I, at some moments await the period, is frequently challenged into a desolating revulsion of every feeling, when I recollect that I must appear in so very humiliating a situation when I reach England! (59)

As she reveals to her friend, despite her calm exterior, she is actually terrified at the prospect of coming to a foreign country as black woman and being forced to marry a stranger. Olivia likens herself to a "state machine," a revealing comparison that means much more than it might at first indicate. On its surface, the phrase suggests that she sees herself as part of her father's larger machinations or plan, one that has political undertones as he seeks to preserve the racial purity of his line at the moment the slave trade had just been abolished. Yet, the definition of "machine" in use at the time has a distinctly material valence that adds an additional layer to Olivia's comparison. Defined as "a mechanical or other structure used for transportation or conveyance,"

---

10   See Dominique, "Introduction," in *The Woman of Colour, A Tale* (Anon), ed. Lyndon J. Dominique (Peterborough: Broadview Press, 2008), 26–7.

and even more granularly as "a military engine," the phrase reveals that Olivia believes that her father's will turns her body into a military machine with an important ideological bent—it is a weapon to combat black encroachment on his bloodline.[11] Like the packets that delivered crucial military intelligence at this period—objects that Olivia's own packets would have travelled alongside—she is "conveyed over the water at the instigation of political contrivance," an automaton weaponized by powers outside of her control.

When she reaches England, Olivia quickly realizes that, despite her wealthy upbringing and education, she has no control over the assumptions and prejudices that people hold regarding the color of her skin; before anyone meets her, they have already "read" her body. Again, like the packets she composes, her body is always already inscribed with political and social meaning that she cannot change; her skin betrays the fact that her father, in accordance with the period's stereotypes about men who lived in the West Indies, copulated with an enslaved African woman. To the English, no matter how "English" Olivia may act, her body reveals the sin through which she was brought into the world. When she walks in public, she writes, "I find I am an object of general curiosity, and many a gentleman follows to repass me, and to be mortified at his folly when he has caught a view of my mulatto countenance" (83). When she attends her first ball in England, she observes that "I was an object of pretty general curiosity, as I entered the room. In such a place as this, the wealth of the Mertons makes them generally known. *My* colour, you know, renders *me* remarkable, and, no doubt, the Clifton world are well acquainted with the particulars of my father's will" (84). Unlike the white people in Clifton society to whom one must speak to in order to learn about them, Olivia's narrative—the circumstances surrounding her birth and her reason for coming to England—is on display from first glance. She likens herself to a visual spectacle, stripped of privacy and bodily autonomy as

> The men [...] walked up in pairs, hanging one on another's arm, and, with a stare of effrontery, eyed your Olivia, as if they had been admitted purposely to see the *untamed savage* at a shilling a piece! While Augustus, was engaged in conversation at a little distance, I head one of these *animals* say to another—"Come, let's have a stare at *Gusty's* black princess!" And with the greatest *sang froid* they *slouched* (for it could not be called walking) up to me; one of them placed his glass most leisurely to his eye, then, shrugging his shoulders, as he looked, he said—"*Pauvre diable!* How I pity him!—a *hundred* thousand wouldn't be enough for the cursed sacrifice!—*Allons Alex.* Let's 'keep moving.' I've had enough—no more—I thank you—quite satisfied, 'pon honour." (85)

---

11   See "machine," n. 3. *OED Online* (Oxford: Oxford University Press, 2020).

As though she were an object in a museum or a circus, the men visually penetrate Olivia's body, audibly remarking on it. They violate her personhood by reducing her to a visual spectacle, reading what they desire onto her flesh and turning her into an object of study and investigation rather than an autonomous subject. To them, her skin is a text to be interpreted, even requiring glasses to better observe her. Like connoisseurs viewing a work of art, they exercise their taste and deem her undesirable. Mirroring the loss of agency she experienced in coming to England in the first place, this moment underscores her profound lack of autonomy over her body within English society, subject to constant interpretation of her skin.

This pattern persists throughout the novel as Augustus eventually decides to marry Olivia and reaches its fever pitch when her marriage and fortune are stripped from her at its dramatic climax. Again, her future is determined by a series of events out of her control, ones that occurred long before she arrived in England. Letitia Merton's plot to reveal Augustus's former wife leaves Olivia distraught and, in the eyes of society, a ruined woman. Her happy future once again ruined by external circumstances—manipulated by others' plots and wills—she takes comfort at least in the fact that "my distresses are not deducible from my own misconduct" (146). Stripped of agency—and never granted any to start with—she embraces her own blamelessness for the bad things that have happened to her. There is the possibility that she will simply become a victim, defined by her innocence and the violence done against her.

Olivia's experience of being "conveyed" like a machine is compounded by the novel's packet structure. While the dangers of the network at this time are never explicitly addressed, she occasionally alludes to the fact that her correspondence with Mrs. Milbanke is mediated by the irregularities of the packet schedule. The transatlantic trade routes that are also responsible for her existence—bringing her enslaved mother to Jamaica—also dictate the terms of her expression. At the end of her first packet to her governess, she breaks off abruptly because "the fleet sails to-morrow; I must therefore, make up my large packet" (93). Later, when we discover Augustus's earlier marriage, we do not immediately learn what impact it has on Olivia because, she writes, "I find I must dispatch this packet" (146), perhaps having received news of a departing boat. In another scene she chalks up her apparent neglect of the correspondence to the irregularities of the service—"As I heard of no ship sailing for Jamaica, I have let my pen lie idle on my standish, my dearest madam, for the last three weeks" (105).

Coupled with these moments in which the structures of the packet network find their way into the narrative, there is at least one instance where we are told a letter is missing from a packet. At the beginning of her second packet, Olivia writes to Mrs. Milbanke, "The hasty lines which I wrote you on the morning that I quitted Clifton, and which you received with my packet, will ere have informed you, that your Olivia has become the wife of her cousin!" (94) The accompanying footnote from the author/editor says that the letter in question "does not appear" (94). While the novel's "editor" consciously omits some of Olivia's words—as I examine next—this case provides no reason for the omission, opening up the possibility that the letter was separated from the rest of her packet, lost at sea, or destroyed. Whatever the case, the noted absence of this extremely important document that announces her marriage emphasizes the material fragility of the packet network and, by extension, Olivia's letters, just at a moment when her future finally seems certain. The missing letter undercuts the levity she expresses at finally, she thinks, knowing what will lie ahead of her. It also calls into question whether her other letters ever reach their destination, and whether others went missing.

In addition to the missing letter scene, the novel's formal instability comes as a result of its pervasive editorial interruptions which serve to formally enact Olivia's sense of not being in control of her own life and story. The author, performing the role of "editor" in the tradition of many "found" eighteenth- and nineteenth-century novels, actively disrupts and undermines the heroine's telling of her own story by making her presence known in the textual spaces between Olivia's letters and by actively removing and editing their contents.[12] The novel's formal markers of editorial intervention, coupled with its packet network context, highlight the mediating forces at work in conveying Olivia's experiences: we get her story not directly but as refracted through both editorial and technological intervention. In the first of these moments, the editor interrupts Olivia's description of her married life with Augustus Merton with the following interjection:

> [In the journal of Olivia, there is at this place a break of some weeks, which the editor laments; as her object in collecting the manuscript has been to portray the character and the sentiments of the Woman of Colour; and hence she has purposely excluded the letters of the other characters in this work: but as, by introducing two of them here, she will be filling a chasm, and letting the reader a little behind the scenes, she makes no apology for their insertion.] (100)

This is the first time we are made aware of the editor's presence. She does not provide a preface or advertisement at the beginning of the novel, which makes her sudden intervention here all the more jarring. The editor "laments" the so-called "break" in Olivia's writings, phrasing that suggests that the editor perhaps bears responsibility for the missing weeks, and not necessarily that Olivia simply took a break from writing. The phrasing also recalls a physical break in the materials, that letters have once again gone missing. Whatever the reason, the editor suddenly makes her presence known in a passage that creates formal dissonance in the narrative and the uncanny feeling that there has been another mediating presence all along. We also learn that other characters besides Olivia have exchanged letters that might otherwise

---

12   Famous examples include Samuel Richardson's novels, Frances Burney's *Evelina* (1778), Walter Scott's *Waverly* (1814), and Mary Shelley's *The Last Man* (1826), as well as many others.

be present in the novel if not for the fact that the editor "purposely excluded" them in order to highlight Olivia's writings. Yet, in pointing out that she has actively excluded some letters, she undermines her own professed elevation of her heroine and calls into question the veracity and authenticity of her narrative. She claims to "fill the chasm" left by the exclusion of Olivia's letters by giving the reader a "behind the scenes" look at what other characters are plotting, but in pulling back the curtain she also reveals that she has been shaping Olivia's narrative all the while, that the heroine has never truly been in command of her story. Just as Olivia is swept along by the whims and decisions of her father and, later, her husband, the editor determines the appearance and form of her personal narrative.

Much later, after Olivia has left Augustus and made a new home for herself and Dido in Wales, the editor again interrupts her packets. The middle of Olivia's fifth packet breaks off between individual letters with the following note: "[As the journal of the ensuing month does not offer any thing which requires insertion, we shall omit it, and go on to a period more material]" (159). The note directly contradicts a passage from Olivia that immediately precedes it, which reads, "No incident occurs, worth relating, the monotonous life which I lead at present, yet I shall not cease to scribble my dear friend" (159). And yet she does stop writing within the novel itself because the editor has excised the "journal of the ensuing month," deeming it inconsequential to the larger story. Olivia's writings are cut from her narrative, leaving yet another gap that calls into question their veracity and authenticity. Her packets are subject to physical manipulation and interpretation just like her body. We are told that the break in her letters covers about a month, but, as in the rest of the novel, her letters are not dated, rendering vague the passage of time. As Olivia's control over her narrative is undercut by the editor's abrupt, intervening presence, it allows the reader to better experience the heroine's feelings of dislocation and insecurity. *The Woman of Colour*'s formal breaks, created by its dominant editorial voice, lack of place names and dates, and occasional missing letters, mimics both Olivia's lack of agency and the precarious circumstances that her correspondence would have experienced on its journey from England to Jamaica.

Olivia's fear that her writings will arrive in Jamaica as a "packet of mutilated scraps" comes true as we learn that the editor has significantly pruned and shaped their contents in constructing a narrative to meet her own purposes: while she fears her letters will be defaced by the material facts of transmission by packet boat, we learn that they are also subject to being disfigured by the material intrusions of the editor (75). In the end, the editor—not Olivia—controls the shape of her narrative life. We learn at the book's conclusion that the editor had a specific purpose all along: to subvert the traditional moral of the marriage plot in which a benevolent heroine is rewarded for her good behavior with a husband. In an odd "dialogue between the editor and a friend" that follows Olivia's final packet, the editor responds to her "friend's" complaint that she has "not rewarded Olivia even with the usual meed of virtue—a husband" by admitting her intended purpose in "editing" the letters:

> Virtue, like Olivia Fairfield's, may truly be said to be its *own reward*— the *moral* I would deduce from her story is, that there is no situation in which the mind ... may not resist itself against misfortune, and become resigned to its fate. And *if* these pages should teach *one child of calamity* to seek *Him* in the hour of distress who is always to be found, if they teach one *skeptical European* to look with a compassionate eye towards the *despised native of Africa*—then, whether Olivia Fairfield's be a *real* or an *imaginary* character, I shall not regret that I have edited the Letters of a *Woman of Colour*! (189)

We learn that the editor's manipulation of Olivia's letters has been in service of her overarching pedagogical goal to teach her readers that virtue is a reward in and of itself, and that having virtue like Olivia allows one to shape one's own future, to "resist" the "misfortune" that happens thanks to uncontrollable circumstances and the whims of others. Olivia's decision at the end of the novel to declare herself a widow and return to Jamaica in order to educate enslaved Africans shows that, despite everything that has happened to her against her will, Olivia refuses to "resign" to her fate and instead "resists" her misfortune, her "virtue" giving her the power to overcome difficulty. She refuses to become a virtuous victim. In addition to offering this philosophy of resistance and rejection of powerlessness, the editor also claims to teach her reader to turn to God in moments of distress and to treat people of color with compassion. Yet it is difficult to take the editor's words at face value after she has repeatedly manipulated Olivia's letters to her purposes, undermining the authority of the person on whose behalf she has advocated. In securing an appropriate moral— even a subversive one for the genre—the editor reframes Olivia's experiences to serve an alternative purpose.

Most readers of the novel agree that, by its end, Olivia manages to obtain a degree of autonomy.[13] As we have seen, when she learns that Augustus is already married and that she has become, in the eyes of her neighbors, a "ruined woman," she decides to declare herself a widow. Although this label appears to defy logic, her decision to self-name in this way harnesses the anti-logic of white English society that has thus far dictated her movements. Nor unlike one of the enslaved insisting upon finding their own name rather than accepting that of the oppressor, so too does Olivia insist upon transvaluing her subject position within society.[14] Taking control of her narrative, of the story people use to name her, Olivia rejects the attempts of those who would

---

13   In addition to those I have already mentioned, Dominique makes this argument in his introduction, writing that "Olivia's most crucial triumph as an independent widow occurs at the end of her narrative when she decides to leave England and return home" (41).

14   On the subject of self-naming as a practice of resistance among the enslaved and people of color,

attempt to delegitimize her after her apparent downfall. In one such moment, a West Indian acquaintance and former travel companion, Mr. Honeywood, learns of the injustices that have befallen her and shows up at her door with an offer of marriage, a move that, if taken, would reinstate Olivia as a respectable member of English society. Although accepting Mr. Honeywood's offer seems the logical choice—one that her maid, Dido, encourages her to make—Olivia refuses him, claiming that she is "not without my resources or my avocations; I can find employment, and I visit my *poor,* though I pass by on the other side of my rich neighbours. I have a sufficiency for all my wants" (162). When he presses her to accept him—knowing full well that no other offers of marriage are likely to come her way and that he has effectively cornered her—she declares,

> "I *now,* and to the *last* moments of my existence, *shall* consider myself the widowed wife of Augustus Merton! [...] My good friend [...] exert your resolution, not let a *woman* be your superior in this quality. I have suffered, Mr. Honeywood, but I have struggled to sustain my sufferings with fortitude, and with consistency of character. Consider my situation, impartially and coolly, and see if I should not suffer in your opinion, were I to act in any way but the one I have fixed on; *that one* which my judgment approves, and which my heart must ever ratify!" (165)

In this bold declaration, Olivia rejects Honeywood's and others' attempts to determine her identity within the proscribed categories which, as a mixed-race woman, she has never quite fit. Rather than becoming a wife once more—a move that would have allowed Honeywood to take legal control of her—she writes herself into a new, impossible category of her own making, the widow of a living man to whom she was never legally married. Justifying this label to Honeywood, she applauds herself for the "fortitude" and "consistency of character" with which she has "sustained" her mistreatment at the hands of forces beyond her control, beginning with the circumstances of her birth and her father's will. Her experience of being "conveyed" by others' wills has apparently given her the strength to make a bid for her own agency, finally assigning herself an identity and purpose based on her own "judgment" and "heart." She rejects the easier, safer option of marrying Honeywood because it would once again deprive her of her autonomy, preferring instead to forge a path of her own. Olivia's achievement of legal autonomy comes as a result of—and not in spite of—the chaotic lack of control she has dealt with up till this point. Embracing the chaos and precarity of her situation is finally what allows her to forge her own way, however illogical, within it.

---

see Rebecca Schneider, "'He says he is free': Narrative Fragments and Self-Emancipation in West Indian Runaway Advertisements," *European Romantic Review* 29 (2018): 435–47.

Yet, read alongside of its editorial instability—coupled with the insecurity of the packet network—the novel's conclusion suggests that Olivia's attempt to control her future may well fail. At the suggestion of Mrs. Milbanke, she and Dido will return home to Jamaica where she will "zealously engage myself in ameliorating the situation, in instructing the minds—in mending the morals of our poor blacks" (188). We also learn that she has regained possession of her father's fortune after a court decision and thus will enjoy fiscal autonomy in her homeland. Still, the continuing context of the packet trade that informs the novel, coupled with its pattern of missing letters, editorial interruptions, and formal inconsistencies, together cast doubt on whether she ultimately achieves this goal. In her final letter, she writes, "my passage is taken in the ****; and to-morrow I set out for Bristol. England, favoured Isle!—Happy country, where the laws are duly administered—where the arts—the sciences flourish, and where religion is to be found in all its beautiful purity. Farewell!—a long farewell!" (188). Instead of ending with her safe arrival in Jamaica, we leave Olivia on the precipice of what we know would have been a dangerous journey, one that we never learn if she safely completes. Her final letter throws into high relief the precariousness of her future and suggests that she and others like her can never be free within the current legal and political system. Instead of hope, the ending's uncertainty promotes a pessimism that offers a condemnation of nineteenth-century society, where even a mixed-race woman as virtuous as Olivia Fairfield suffers mistreatment because of her race and gender. Olivia's farewell to England—which she calls "a place where laws are duly administered" and "where religion is to be found"—comes across as bitingly ironic in light of her abuse at the hands of an unfair legal system that has regarded her as little more than property. The reader, left at the close of the novel in the kind of uncertainty Olivia lives every day, might see beyond all potential happy endings to the distinctly unhappy beginnings and middles that mark the lives of women of color. *The Woman of Colour* draws upon the precarity and political importance of the packet network in order to harshly critique the nation it served.

https://doi.org/10.3828/eir.2020.27.2.5

Counting the Bodies: Ferguson and Ferguson[1]

Bakary Diaby
Skidmore College

1958 saw the release of one of Patsy Cline's most famous songs, "If I could See the World (Through the Eyes of a Child)."[2] In it, Cline croons how "wonderful [a] world this would be" should she have such a childlike understanding of the world; it would show her a world with "no trouble and no strife [...] / [and] a bluebird in every tree." The song's conceit relies on a model of childhood unencumbered by the weight of identity or of having a body. Unfortunately, of course, not all children perceive the world the same way. The world's "wonder" is contingent on material conditions that different children experience in different ways.

The song suggests that the complex issues of the world can somehow be simplified. Such a political project often underpins artwork focalized around children. The 2016 exhibit ... *when they grow up* ... by Ebony G. Patterson, however, breaks the mold. Patterson makes perceptible the ways in which the material conditions of modern life intersect with childhood by joining together racial violence on the one hand with the power of the aesthetic on the other. But unlike Cline's song, Patterson questions how children are perceived rather than how children perceive, especially when the latter process is colored by innocence and ignorance. For example, while resting on a soft pink carpet, primed to see innocence and ease, the viewer is instead confronted with Black children riddled with bullet holes.[3]

---

1   The author thanks Isaac Cowell, Greg Ellermann, William Galperin, Erin Goss, Colin Jager, Carter Mathes, and Michelle Speitz for feedback and encouragement at various stages of this essay's development. I also wish to express particular gratitude to the efforts of Alexander Schlutz, Alan Vardy, and the editors of *Essays in Romanticism* for their helpful insight and generous feedback. This research was assisted by a Mellon/ACLS Dissertation Completion Fellowship from the American Council of Learned Societies.

2   Patsy Cline, "If I could See the World (Through the Eyes of a Child)," Decca Records, 1958.

3   I capitalize "Black" when referring to people of African descent. As a proper noun, the word designates a social identity with a long, global history. In 1930, after a campaign led by W. E. B. Du Bois, the New York Times began to capitalize "Negro" as "an act in recognition of racial respect for those who have been generations in the 'lower case.'" While scholars and linguists have made a similar claim for "Black" for decades, many style guides still urge writers to leave the first letter lowercase, arguing that "black" refers to a color and is an adjectival modifier (of, for example, "black Americans"). In fact, *The New York Times Manual of Style and Usage* recommended the lowercase "black" when referring to "African-Americans" only until July of 2020. That said, the word should be capitalized to match proper grammar. As Lori Tharps observed, "The Associated Press also

Here are individuated children who symbolize collective racial violence. While Patterson's models are living, ... *when they grow up* ... has them stand for countless slain Black lives. Made in the wake of the murder of Black children—and women, and men, and the gender nonconforming—it is hard not to think of Tamir Rice or Aiyana Stanley-Jones when one sees Patterson's art. That is, in spite of the vibrant colors, the smiling faces, and the littered-about toys, it is hard not to think of death. This is a picture of life, but a melancholy picture of life. And while it strives to address (or redress) Stacey Patton's too-true contention that "in America, Black children don't get to be children," the artist's insistence on the value of Black life operates against the backdrop of mass death the piece invokes.[4] Such mass death forms the necropolitical ground upon which Black Lives Matter stands, a "movement [that] can be read as an attempt to keep mourning an open dynamic in our culture because black lives exist in a state of precariousness."[5]

I will return to my characterization of these images as a "melancholy picture of life" at the end of this essay. But my main concern is counting not only the dead, but also counting the living. To do so, I connect the two "Fergusons" of my title: Frances Ferguson and Ferguson, Missouri, which functions here as a stand-in for present day "race relations" in the United States. Starting with Frances Ferguson's *Solitude and the Sublime: Romanticism and the Aesthetics of Individuation* (1992), I lay the groundwork for describing the Romantic politics of "counting." Ferguson's work, however, has not been applied to Black Lives Matter or to Africana Studies in general. I hope to lay the groundwork for ways in which Romantic aesthetics can be put in a mutually constructive dialogue with afropessimist thought. Rather than using one to criticize the other, I aim to show how these two seemingly disparate intellectual formations are parallel beams supporting racial issues of the present. And further, I will contend that an analysis of Romanticism's political stakes should make use of the idealism central to it, and that such a use does not attenuate the urgency or efficacy of Romanticist work.

My title carries three possible meanings, and those meanings mark how I structure this essay. In the first section, I discuss aesthetically counting those who die because of systemic moral failure. This part of my paper looks at the use of enumeration within artistic media bound up with social justice. In the subsequent section, I expound on the connections between making bodies "count" and making them "matter." The link between accumulation and materiality possesses a history steeped in anti-blackness and a present directed towards anti-racist action. I use Ferguson's own analysis of the semiotics of counting—and the attendant issues of materiality such semiotics

---

decrees that the proper names of 'nationalities, peoples, races, tribes' should be capitalized. What are Black people, then?"

4   Stacy Patton, "In America, Black Children Don't Get to be Children," *Washington Post*, 26 November 2014.

5   Claudia Rankine, "The Condition of Black Life is One of Mourning," *New York Times*, 22 June 2015.

engender—to elaborate on this history and present.[6] In my final section, I turn to Romanticism to think about how one body can "count" for others. I end with William Wordsworth's "We are Seven," a lyric featuring a child very much—on the surface—akin to the unmarked idealized one of Cline's song. "We are Seven" is, in Ferguson's words, the "most frequently mocked poem by the most frequently parodied writer in English."[7] My guiding question is this: what political possibilities arise when we take *this* poem seriously?

The Aesthetics of the Omitted

For Enlightenment thinkers, "aesthetics" referred to a science of sensation, a study of the connection between perception and pleasure (and for Shaftesbury, Kant, and others, moral action). Now, contemporary scholars use it to unify affect, cognitive acts, and socio-economic analysis—or "politics" *in toto*—into a single philosophical inquiry. Take, for instance, *The Politics of Aesthetics* (2000, 2004) where Jacques Rancière expands aesthetics—the root of which means "sensing"—to be at the very heart of the political. For Rancière, politics is an "aesthetic" concern since it "revolves around what is seen and what can be said about it, around who has the ability to see and the talent to speak."[8] Aesthetics, in short, point to the perceptible and to why anything or anyone is, has been, or is not perceptible. A subject assuming the universality of his subjective judgments and extrapolating them to others extends his own prejudices and ignorances onto others as well. This false assumption reproduces structural inequalities, and an expanding aesthetics of omission.

Many politically activist contemporary artists tackle this kind of aesthetic inequality. Speaking on Ebony G. Patterson's work, for example, Patricia Joan Saunders remarks that "one of the ways contemporary art has been an effective tool for social justice is through its capacity to entice viewers into a more considered mode of looking."[9] As with … *when they grow up* …, "what makes her work distinct is that it provides us with a unique occasion to map political landscapes as well as technologies of representation and oppression" (102). Put simply, Patterson's work disrupts not only *what* we sense but also *how* we perceive others. An ethical element of aesthetics entails breaking habits of representation that contribute to oppression and obstruction, providing audiences with an opportunity to adopt a "more considered mode" of understanding the Other.

---

6   Ferguson's chapter on Godwin and population is another direct link, but the ties between society on the one hand and counting on the other in that chapter would limit me to counting-as-enumeration and not counting-as-mattering. I am interested in the discourse of materiality given its contemporary racial resonance.

7   Frances Ferguson, *Solitude and the Sublime: The Romantic Aesthetics of Individuation* (New York: Routledge, 1992), 164.

8   Jacques Rancière, *The Politics of Aesthetics: The Distribution of the Sensible,* trans. Gabriel Rockhill (London: Bloomsbury Academic, 2004), 8 (emphasis added).

9   Patricia Joan Saunders, "Gardening in the Garrisons, You Never Know What You Will Find: (Un)visibility in the Works of Ebony G. Patterson," *Feminist Studies* 42, no. 1 (2016): 98.

The goal of better perceiving the Other is moot, however, if audiences are willfully unaware of the Other and the depths of their suffering. As with the difficulty Marissa Fuentes encountered when telling the stories of enslaved women in Barbados, the "challenge" lies in "writ[ing] a history about what an archive does not offer."[10] Below, I discuss two art objects that perform the aesthetic project of scrutinizing our habits of perception and representation, one by Claudia Rankine (b. 1963) and another by Alfredo Jaar (b. 1956). If "history is produced from what the archive offers," then these art objects challenge the limitations of both history and its archive to value and (re)present Black suffering (146).

In *Citizen: An American Lyric* (2014), her somber, multi-media meditation on Blackness and everyday racism, Claudia Rankine continues to list the dead. One page lists the names of Black women and men unjustly killed, often by police officers. Opposite the page, the speaker explains: "because white men can't / police their imagination / black men are dying."[11] With subsequent printings, Rankine adds more names, and the writing on the stark white page becomes lighter and lighter. The names add up because the killings do not stop. *Citizen* is a living text because we keep dying.

The fade into whiteness implies that the list continues *ad infinitum*. That it continues dramatizes the effacement of these people's lives and their deaths. Rankine's fading page does not only attempt to immortalize the names it bears, it also immortalizes the constant forgetting of these names, of these people. This page in *Citizen* exemplifies how an artist strives to bring to better understanding the racist strictures of modern life by counting those who die. One finds a similar logic at play in "untitled (Newsweek)," a part of Alfredo Jaar's larger *The Rwanda Project, 1994–2000*. Like Rankine's page it too counts the dead. In so doing, it endeavors to bring a genocide and its obfuscation into better visibility.

Jaar juxtaposes descriptions of the events leading to and during the Rwandan genocide with images of that week's *Newsweek* cover.[12] The covers appear after a short delay, emphasizing the often bathetic payoff of *Newsweek*'s feature headline. On a slide, for instance, detailing the reduction of United Nations peacekeeping forces just as the killings became more frequent, we see the *Newsweek* cover on "The Search for the Magic Pill Better than Vitamins." Each of the verbal descriptions on the left end with a growing tally of the dead. The first *Newsweek* cover featuring Rwanda appears after a million people have already been killed and four million more displaced. Then, the slides end.

Counting like this can inform an audience of a tragedy that is sublime in its scope. But the strategy of counting or listing here does not aestheticize the tragedy per se but

10   Marisa J. Fuentes, *Dispossessed Lives: Enslaved Women, Violence, and the Archive* (Philadelphia: University of Pennsylvania Press, 2016), 146.

11   Claudia Rankine, *Citizen: An American Lyric* (Minneapolis: Graywolf Press, 2014), 135. Notably, not all of the listed victims are "men," since Sandra Bland was added in a later printing.

12   The project is still available on Jaar's website. It can be found at http://www.alfredojaar.net/rwanda_web/95newsweek/newsweek.html.

rather the inattention to and/or the immutability of it. In point of fact, the "overall sense of *The Rwanda Project*," for Sue Marais, "is of the inadequacy of both visual and verbal codes of representation ... to encompass the enormity of genocide."[13] And yet, "untitled (Newsweek)" consists entirely of visual images and verbal descriptions of the atrocity.

With the eventual inclusion of the genocide in *Newsweek's* coverage, Jaar acknowledges that these victims—millions of Tutsi, Twa, and moderate Hutus—ultimately became grievable lives in the West. But such a "pretense of grief" for the killed and the survivors winds up being "a failure of representation," since, in the words of Nicholas Mirzoeff, "it attempts to cover up the wider failure to engage with the questions of colonization, decolonization, and globalization that led ... to Rwanda's genocide" in the first place.[14] If, as Michael Levan describes, Jaar's installations are a "fold[ing] together [of] complex questions of political trauma, habits of representation and ... visibility," then part of the aesthetic project here is to disrupt those habits.[15] The strategies both *Citizen* and "untitled (Newsweek)" employ to break those habits are key to my argument here.

Those strategies are easy to glean: Rankine lists, and Jaar tallies; listing and tallying appear to be simple tasks. However, such tasks in these contexts impugn the famous (and often erroneously attributed) aphorism that "one death is a tragedy, but a million deaths are a statistic." This is not because of empathetic readers or viewers. Rather, these artworks succeed in pointing to shared ignorance, social imperceptibility, and indirect culpability.

Rankine lists, and Jaar tallies. Both find political utility in/via aesthetic matters. But the logic that undergirds both is, I suggest, a mix of the "Romantic" and the afropessimist. The logic draws from the Romantic in how it seeks to imbue the immaterial (e.g. one's personhood) with social worth. This is also a central component of the goals of Black Lives Matter, which we can see in the very name. As for the latter, the logic here mirrors the "stringent argument of afro-pessimist theory [...] that to inhabit black positionality, is already to be an object rather than a subject."[16] This argument is manifest in both the too-long ungrieved suffering of the Rwandan victims and in the overdetermined "danger" of the Black body. The afropessimist character of Rankine's list also draws from the long American history of intertwining race, cumulation, and death. In Frank Wilderson's words, with slavery, "from the very beginning, we were meant to be accumulated and die."[17] Iyko Day further historicizes this dynamic:

---

13   Sue Marais, "'The Economies of Repetition': The Market, the Artistic, and the Genocidal in Ivan Vladislavić's 'Curiouser,'" *The Journal of Commonwealth Literature* 52, no. 1 (2017): 35.

14   Nicholas Mirzoeff, "Invisible Again: Rwanda and Representation After Genocide," *African Arts* 38, no. 3 (2005): 91.

15   Michael Levan, "Folding Trauma: On Alfredo Jaar's Installations and Interventions," *Performance Research* 16, no. 1 (2011): 82.

16   Nathan Brown, "The Irony of Anatomy: Basquiat's Poetics of Black Positionality," *Radical Philosophy* 195 (2016): 17.

17   Frank Wilderson, "Gramsci's Black Marx: Whither the Slave in Civil Society," *Social Identities* 9, no. 2 (2003): 238.

Given that emancipated African Americans were neither "immigrants" who could be deported nor a population that could be eliminated through biological absorption, African Americans became an undisposable alien labor population, which accounts for the intensity through which subsequent generations of African Americans have been subject to a logic of exclusion where the only means of disposal is death.[18]

Rankine extends this to the present in "The Condition of Black Life is one of Mourning," noting how "dead blacks are a part of normal life here. Dying in ship hulls, tossed into the Atlantic, hanging from trees, beaten, shot in churches, gunned down by the police or warehoused in prisons" (Rankine, "Condition"). The issue at hand, then, is how to decouple quotidian Black death from indifference. That is, with so many deaths, how do we make each one matter?

Bodies that Count

Frances Ferguson's *Solitude and the Sublime* binds Romantic aesthetics' concern with "counting" to this related concept of "mattering." In her chapter on Wordsworth and "We Are Seven," Ferguson deconstructs the breakdown of the semiotic "coordination of meaning" in the Romantic period. The "convergence of [certain systematizing] uses of number in the late eighteenth century suggests the possibility of reading a poem like 'We Are Seven,'" she suggests, "in terms of a more general movement to coordinate meanings among individuals" (Ferguson 169). As such, the Romantics altered the relationship between signs (like names and numbers) on the one hand and the material world they theoretically refer to on the other. Ferguson discusses two types of the disintegration between signs and referents, one exemplified by Kantian Formalism and another latent in literary theory, exemplified by the work of Paul de Man and Jerome McGann. While de Man and McGann work with very different notions of materiality, Ferguson argues that "they both resolve interpretative issues in favor of an insistence on a more explicit (McGann) and a more covert (de Man) empiricism" (168). She contests their hermeneutic empiricism with an idealist response. So, where poststructuralism saw "a gap" between name and referent, "the understanding of mathematics … associated with Kant sees an interval" (169). The difference between a "gap" and an "interval" is subtle but significant. First, it differentiates "numbering from number" (168). In the latter case, order is paramount. The former allows fungibility, encouraging a kind of ontic equivalence in the items being counted. Also, rather than a lack, Kantian idealist semiology posits that "the patterning of language [is] at least as important as its ostensible referents" (169). Thus, Romantic formalism "rescues language from a fundamental empiricism … by making

---

18   Iyko Day, *Alien Capital: Asian Racialization and the Logic of Settler Colonial Capitalism* (Durham: Duke University Press, 2016), 29.

it clear that the relationships among [signifiers] supplements empirical reference" instead of being dependent on it (169).

According to Ferguson, this idealist semiology stands apart from de Man's own conception of the relationship between materiality and phenomenality. She asserts that for de Man, the former sets the condition of possibility for the latter: "materiality … [is] the stuff of language before it is appropriated to perception." In her reading of his chapter on Rousseau's *Confessions* in *Allegories of Reading* (1979), Ferguson argues that de Man saw "materiality as necessary to language" and subsequently made the mistake of seeing "materiality as exclusively constitutive of language" (156). His mistake produces a circular semiotic system where "matter without meaning makes the production of meaning possible" (158).

Working from Ferguson's formalist account of Romantic semiology, "matter" adopts two competing meanings. Both are present in anti-racist struggle in the present. First, the discourse of physical and symbolic racist violence attempts to make mere matter out of minority social groups, reducing them to objects. To be more specific, it is the violence and trauma of white supremacy itself that "[w]hite supremacy tries to reduce people of color to."[19] The Black body, for example, becomes a memorial to historical violence, present-day suffering, and the ineluctable fate of all living things to die. People of color metonymically recall violence so much so that we become accustomed to the suffering Black—or Brown, Latinx, Asian, or indigenous—body. Saidiya Hartman tried to resist this state of affairs by not quoting the famous beating scene from Douglass's *Narrative* in her profoundly influential study, *Scenes of Subjection* (1997). For Hartman, the "ease with which" racial violence "reinforces the spectacular character of black suffering" can become a kind of "narcissistic identification that obliterates the other."[20] These scenes, "rather than inciting indignation," frequently "immure us to pain by virtue of their familiarity" (3).

But there is another sense of "matter" at play here, the same used in the expression "Black Lives Matter." This sense of "matter" operates—ironically—in the immaterial and links materiality with value. Usefully, the "Romantic and specifically Kantian idealism" Ferguson discusses advances an aesthetics of matter where the "material" is not co-extensive with the perceptible (Ferguson viii). Such a Romantic significatory system would help to reconcile the meanings of divergent "way[s] of conceiving persons," the core of the crisis of meaning in the eighteenth century.

If Ferguson is right about signification in the Romantic period, then anti-racist possibility resides in disputing divergent "way[s] of conceiving persons." Or rather, in this case, the issue at hand is more about divergent ways of representing and perceiving vulnerable or marginalized persons. For example, the meaning of "images of the pained black body," according to Debra Walker King, is fashioned

---

19 Jenny Zhang, "They Pretend to be Us While Pretending We Don't Exist," *BuzzFeed* (2015), http://bzfd.it/2vJ8AeH.
20 Saidiya V. Hartman, *Scenes of Subjection: Terror, Slavery, and Self-Making in Nineteenth-Century America* (Oxford: Oxford University Press, 1997), 3, 4.

"through ongoing 'conversations' between normalizing cultural politics and ... individual [subjects'] negotiations of how they can or will accept [those] normalizing paradigms."[21] Art often mediates such conversations, as I suggested above in regards to Patterson, Rankine, and Jaar. Since language is no longer trapped in a one-to-one relationship with the material world, the interval between language and world allows art to say something "in an incomprehensible language" that may still be understood by audiences nonetheless (Ferguson 168). We can learn to resist and oppose images that habituate us to the suffering of others because art triggers what Rancière has called a *dissensus*, a "dispute of the given." Romantic idealism is not a rejection of the "material" or an escape from the perceptible. Rather, it augments the sensible and does not take "the given" for granted.

I will argue below that Wordsworth's "We are Seven" encapsulates this Romantic idealism in the way it strives to personify persons, to figure the figurative and thereby render it more dear. And further, the poem achieves this through "counting." I must first, however, qualify Ferguson's Romantic idealism since putting it in dialogue with afropessimist thought would hold that it remains implicitly limited by race. Perhaps, that is, her personified persons are white and, using European idealist thought, can only ever be. This is because afropessimism takes "claims of universal humanity" to be "hobbled by a ... contradiction that manifests whenever one looks seriously at the structure of Black suffering in comparison to the presumed universal structure of all sentient beings."[22] According to Frank Wilderson, "afropessimism argues [that] Blacks are not Human subjects, but are instead structurally inert props" (14). It posits Blackness not as an identity per se but rather as a "structural position of noncommunicability in the face of all other positions," as the counterbalance to identities formed within Eurocentric modernity.[23] For Wilderson, idealism—including, then, its Romantic variant—would thus be part of "the entire world's semantic field ... sutured together by anti-Black solidarity" (58). It would follow then that arriving at personhood via idealist accounting binds us to an ideal/material binary informed by racial difference. This is so because "Idealism's other" is not solely materialism writ large but, as Jared Hickman argued, "the fetish-worshiping African whose supposed mental enslavement is made a justification or explanation for his physical enslavement."[24] Hegel "facilitated his opposition of Africa to the Absolute" by building on and advancing both secular and theological binaries pitting advancement against African primitivism (117, 125). Afropessimism would point to this complicity as reason enough for idealism's inability to meaningfully make Black lives matter.

21   Debra Walker King, *African Americans and the Culture of Pain* (Charlottesville: University of Virginia Press, 2008), 31.
22   Frank B. Wilderson, *Afropessimism* (New York: Liveright, 2020) 14.
23   Frank B. Wilderson, *Red, White & Black: Cinema and the Structure of U.S. Antagonisms* (Durham: Duke University Press, 2010), 58.
24   Jared Hickman, *Black Prometheus: Race and Radicalism in the Age of Atlantic Slavery* (New York: Oxford University Press, 2017), 117.

So even though "counting" names a Romantic process of personifying persons, its idealist roots mean that, to some, it remains incapable of integrating Black positionality. While it is true that turning to idealism brings with it this limitation that afropessimism would ascribe to it, I will still maintain that the Romantic logic of personifying persons remains at play in afropessimist work, even if that work is refuting such logic or detailing its impossibility in quotidian praxis. My aim here is to provide Romanticism with no alibi; instead, I turn to Romantic idealism to consider how a capacity to "unrealize" a reality built on injustice can complement the materialist concerns of afropessimism.[25]

Many in One Body

To further explore that dynamic between Romantic idealism and afropessimist materialism, I turn to William Wordsworth's "We Are Seven." In what follows, I practice a reading of the poem that delineates and develops the interpretive and political utility of Romantic counting. This reading is, admittedly, an idealistic one in multiple senses of the word. But it suggests the possibility of a political Romanticism that leans into its idealizing, not as a substitute for material concerns but as a means to bolster our engagement with the devaluing of vulnerable lives.

In the poem, the speaker recalls to "dear brother Jem" a conversation he once had with an eight-year-old girl. For a reason never explicitly stated, he desires to know more about the girl's family, including the number of her siblings. Upon learning that two of the seven have passed away, the speaker declares, then, that there are five siblings whereas the girl insists upon there still being seven of them.

In *Romantic Things*, Mary Jacobus argues that this poem asks "what should lyric poetry know of death, when the lyric has so much to do with life?"[26] The lyric is indeed a form that presupposes animation of some kind. But this simple poem also poses the question of what or who "counts" as a person and why: how do we differentiate five living children from seven people? And one final question: just why does this speaker care so much?

We can turn to Hollis Robbins for an answer to that question.[27] Robbins notes the close similarity of the speaker's questions to the first British census, showing how the poem overlaps the bureaucratic and the poetic. Together with Ferguson's interpretation—that the poem is "tak[ing] up the question of personification"—this suggests that the girl can personify her siblings even as she cannot change the speaker and reader's views that they have lost their status as legal persons of the state (164).

25   I take the word "unrealize" from Coleridge. In a letter most likely from 1816, Coleridge remarks how since "childhood I have been accustomed to *abstract* and as it were unrealize whatever of more than common interest my eyes dwelt on." This is from letter 167 in the second volume of the *Biographia Epistolaris* (1911).

26   Mary Jacobus, *Romantic Things: A Tree, a Rock, a Cloud* (Chicago; London: The University of Chicago Press, 2012), 115.

27   Hollis Robbins, "'We Are Seven' and the First British Census," *English Language Notes* 48, no. 2 (2010): 201–13.

Ferguson observed that "critics have tended to defend the child and abuse the man" (165). Some read his assertions as a domineering naive realism. Ferguson's recuperation of the adult speaker sees his eventual departure (and perhaps too his eventual relating of the story) as a sign that he has understood the girl's intent; in lieu of a "debate," then, Ferguson sees a reconciliation of divergent ways of conceiving persons. Thus, the poem becomes "a representation in miniature of the spirit animating paraphrase … in which the coordination of meaning counts neither as oppression nor as formal accident" (169). Here, "counting" serves as the mechanism to coordinate meaning. The man understands by the end of the dialogue that counting assumes "references that are available to be pointed to" (165). But while he may get her point, the issue becomes what he can do with this information. If the speaker does in fact resemble (or might even be) a census employee, then he would be looking to ascertain "the number of *persons*, excluding soldiers and sailors, found in the parish on the day of inquiry."[28] So if he does represent a kind of bureaucratic sense of (ac)counting, then her siblings still fail to count in official capacities. That is, even if he "gets" it, he will still have to report five children and the little girl becomes a tale to share with "Dear brother Jem" (the only named character who is still alive) about a lonely idealizing child stranded in a harsh material world. Thus, "for the man, what is there now is what counts" (Ferguson 165).

What is more, like her dead siblings, she herself does not "count." Asked "Where [each of her brothers and sisters] are," she responds:

> … two of us at Conway dwell,
> And two are gone to sea.
>
> Two of us in the churchyard lie,
> My sister and my brother,
> And in the church-yard cottage, I
> Dwell near them with my mother. (ll. 19–24)[29]

The fact that she lives "in the church-yard cottage" reveals that she comes from a family dependent on the local parish. In other words, she hails from either the lower-middle class or the poor. And since the father is never mentioned, failing to appear in a list the girl gives that included her mother, probability suggests the latter.[30] But the crucial

---

28   Quoted in Robbins, 204 (emphasis added).

29   William Wordsworth, *The Major Works Including the Prelude* (Oxford: Oxford University Press, 2008), 83, http://www.pcfleming.com/wp-content/uploads/2014/06/We-Are-Seven-4.jpg.

30   Though is it strange that the father is never counted, even if he, as we can presume, died. He may have been one of Wordsworth's many male characters who desert their family for one reason or another. But if so, he would differ from four of her siblings who she still lists despite being physically absent (two went to Conwy, and two have died). And while there is nothing to confirm whether "little Jane" is older than her, the girl in the poem is probably not the youngest since she seems to remember seeing "little Jane … / In bed … moaning" (ll. 49–50). If so, and the mother conceived another child

detail in the lines quoted above is the definite article before the word "church-yard." The article points to a particular place that locals—and perhaps even the speaker—would know. Furthermore, they would know what living there implies. Local parishes for small villages were held responsible for the poor in their communities from 1601 until 1834, including their housing.[31] Many indigent families ended up living in "church-yard cottages" like the young child in the poem (l. 23). The dole such families received "were … equivalent perhaps to the wages of a boy laborer" (241). And if her family did manage to receive a dole, then it would have to be divided among at least two people (241).[32] This "little cottage girl" is a poetic version of the destitute children depicted in Thomas Gainsborough's *Cottage Girl with Dog and Pitcher* (1785) or *Cottage Children* (1787), popular images of vulnerability in the period. In short, she is not just any random rural child but an extremely poor one. And despite the obviousness of her acutely straitened circumstances—the speaker describes her as having a "rustic, woodland air" and being "wildly clad"—the full brunt of this fact remains under-explored in the critical literature of "We Are Seven" (ll. 9–10).

Because of her status as a parish child, this young girl does not "count" in the eyes of the British state for very much at all. Despite this, she "counts" for others in two senses of the term: (1) she can include her dead siblings into the realm of the sensible for the speaker and the reader (i.e. she counts them and thus can account *for* them) and (2) she stands in substitutively for others (i.e. she can count for them). The poem details how the marginalized can operate on a model of personhood not congruent to or even compatible with that of the state.

The "purpose" Wordsworth assigned to "We Are Seven" in the 1802 "Preface" on the other hand, seems patently inexact. The "feelings and ideas" in the poem supposedly concern "the perplexity and obscurity which in childhood attend our notion of death, or, rather our utter inability to admit that notion" (Wordsworth 598). But the young girl engages in no casuistry, subterfuge, or sophistry. She simply tries to answer the speaker's questions truthfully. Frances Ferguson reads the child's reply of "We Are Seven" in response to the speaker as, from the standpoint of the child, no different than a casual riposte like "I am seven" to answer the question "how old are you" (Ferguson 164)? For Ferguson, "the fact of her being seven in being one is to her as readily apparent as the fact that she has thick curly hair" (164–5). It is just another constitutive element of her personhood.

---

after the daughter in the poem, why does the young girl omit her father? Another likely scenario would suggest that the father is a vagrant farmer, who goes wherever he can find work. The Poor Laws (specifically the 1536 Act and the 1601 statute itself) empowered parishes to take in the children of vagrant workers and other poor families (even against their consent) in order "to set [them] to work and apprentice[ships]" (O'Day 244). He might be so infrequent a presence in her life that it results in his omission. Nonetheless, any of these possibilities make evident that the girl here comes from a very indigent background.

31   Rosemary O'Day, *Education and Society, 1500–1800: The Social Foundations of Education in Early Modern Britain* (Oxford: Longman, 1982), 244.

32   That is, the girl and her mother.

Moreover, Wordsworth must have seen that she in fact does "admit" the notion of death. There is no reticence, "perplexity," or "obscurity" at all when she informs the speaker that "The first that *died* was little Jane" (emphasis added, l. 49). Rather than "confused" or in denial about the deaths, this child re-values their lives and their afterlives. With both characters staying in the present tense, the repeated insistence on how many siblings there are now means that these children "count" in a way up for debate. The speaker subscribes to the model of counting most likely shared by the reader in holding that the dead do not count. But the girl suggests the possibility of being otherwise, urging the better angels of our nature to conceive a being-in-the-world where death is different in degree but not in kind from going to Conwy. I claimed above, following Ferguson, that Romantic counting is predicated on an idea of numbers, signs, and names that augments empirical reference rather than limits it or is limited by it. Thus, "if names such as Jane and John ... enable one to represent persons as existing even when they cannot be seen," then names allow us to "insist upon the existence of those names beyond their" lost referents (165).

This girl possesses little power in the eyes of the government of Great Britain in 1793—when Wordsworth may have met a child like this or found a grave marked "We Are Seven"—or in 1797–98 during the walking tour when he composed the poem. She is decidedly poor, female, a minor, and possibly Welsh, rendered subaltern in numerous ways. And yet, the "simple child" affirms her autonomy to personify lost or forgotten people. In performing this kind of personification, she offers a way to change the criteria by which we "value" each other. More importantly, the poem implicitly challenges the reader to do the same. The criteria no longer rest on living and presence or the inclusion in the state's tabulations.

The principal conflict here encompasses the problematics of personifying persons so that they "matter" by the second sense I offered above. For this young girl is a Romantic subject for whom dignity defeats death. The child in "We Are Seven" reaffirms the dignity of the poor and, with it, the right to be valued. She provides a case for imaginative response to state power and permits us to revel in the fantastic.

She replies to the speaker with a poetic answer that tries to give an account of oneself and proves that no subject is only ever herself. We can all be seven—or any number—in being one. As Judith Butler describes Foucault's later work in *Giving an Account of Oneself*, the "subject forms itself ... in ways that not only (a) reveal self-constitution to be a kind of *poiesis* but (b) establish self-making as part of the broader operation of critique."[33] *Poiesis* and critique are, in "We Are Seven," the foundations of a Romantic selfhood that does not limit itself—in any way—to the body, to presence, or to the juridical absolutism of counting that is endemic to bureaucratic statistics. The poetic genesis of the Romantic subject highlights a way of counting the discounted and the dead, a counting that acts as a model of idealist political critique.

---

33   Judith Butler, *Giving an Account of Oneself* (New York: Fordham University Press, 2005), 17.

This falls in line with Ian Baucom's notion of "melancholy realism," a decidedly "romantic ... form of existence."[34] This "romantic type," that is, the melancholy realist, "implicitly resists the exchange of life for death by seeking to return dead things to life and insisting on the affective reality of the ... ghosts it calls" forth (46). Melancholy realism fictions the dead and the uncounted back into meaningfulness. In short, it manipulates death to make lives (and living) matter. Returning to Ebony G. Patterson's ... *when they grow up* ... and my description of its main wall as a melancholy picture of life, I meant to call it a melancholy *fictioning* of life, a Romantic resistance against the "exchange of life for death" and death for life; each child stands in for the *lives* of countless others, not only their deaths.

To call Patterson's work "Romantic," however, would be a laden charge and I refuse to do so here. But the baggage of such a charge, I would wager, stems from ... *when they grow up* ... and Patterson's work in general being "political." Implied, then, is the claim that Romantic aesthetics, to many outside the field, can*not* be political, or is political in the worst ways. Romanticism's aestheticizing seems more than *a*politcal when addressing issues like contemporary racial violence, it proves disastrously *anti*-political. This assumes, however, that the aesthetic and its connection to art and unreality negate and repel the political. I have insisted in turn that the idealizing and aestheticizing impulses of the melancholy realist need not be solipsistic moonshine. As Sharon Patricia Holland notes, "Fantasy ... can oscillate between delusion and creative hope."[35] This essay has been, to some degree, a defense of "creative hope," of Romantic aestheticizing and melancholy realism. If anything, I am suggesting that one does not need to run into the austere arms of an over-simplified materialism in order to imbue Romanticism with "political" stakes. There will always be crucial work in attending to the material conditions of life and death; I have done some of that work here and I will continue to do so in the future. But in these times, there is also room for idealism, room for romance, and room, then, for Romanticism.

---

34   Ian Baucom, *Specters of the Atlantic: Finance Capital, Slavery, and the Philosophy of History* (Durham: Duke University Press, 2005), 46.
35   Sharon Patricia Holland, *The Erotic Life of Racism* (Durham: Duke University Press, 2012), 4.

STUDIES
IN
ROMANTICISM

**Annual Individual
Subscriptions**
$30.00 *(print)*;
$35.00 *(online)*

**Annual Institutional
Subscriptions**
$80.00 *(print)*;
$80.00 *(online)*;
$112.00 *(print & online)*

Adriana Craciun, *Editor*
Joseph Rezek, *Associate Editor*

BOSTON UNIVERSITY

Studies in Romanticism is the flagship journal of Romantic literary studies. Edited at Boston University since its founding there in 1961, *SiR* has been committed to advancing the study of literature and culture in the dynamic "Romantic Century" of 1750-1850. International in sympathies and interdisciplinary in approaches, *SiR* publishes the highest caliber scholarship on British, Anglophone, and European Romantic-era studies from diverse methodological perspectives.

Published 4 times per year in April, July, October, and January. Volume 60 (2021).
P-ISSN: 0039-3762; E-ISSN: 2330-118X.

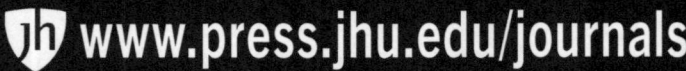

https://doi.org/10.3828/eir.2020.27.2.6

Byron's Cosmopolitan "East"

Joey S. Kim
University of Toledo

While cantos I and II of *Childe Harold's Pilgrimage* (1812) inaugurated Byron's celebrity, it was the Eastern Tales that followed—*The Giaour* (1813), *The Bride of Abydos* (1813), *The Corsair* (1814), and *Lara* (1814)—that garnered him popular literary acclaim. Multiple editions and reprints of these four tales turned Byron into not only a literary brand name but also a celebrated Orientalist. Byron may have famously parodied himself in *Beppo* (1817)—writing "How quickly would I print (the world delighting) / A Grecian, Syrian, or Assyrian tale; / And sell you, mix'd with western sentimentalism, / Some samples of the finest Orientalism!" (4: 405–8)—but this ironic distance was produced in part by the unprecedented sales of the Eastern Tales.[1] For Byron, Orientalist trends came at a specifically opportune time in his career.[2] While working on *The Giaour*, the first of his Eastern Tales, he wrote a letter to Thomas Moore instructing him to "stick to the East," for "the public are Orientalizing."[3] Byron followed his own advice, publishing *The Bride of Abydos*, *The Corsair*, and *Lara* over the course of the next year.

Prior to the tales, *Childe Harold's Pilgrimage* cemented Byron's poetic subjectivity as a type of cosmopolitan brand.[4] The *Le Cosmopolite* epigraph to *Childe Harold's Pilgrimage* compares the "universe" to a "sort of book whose first page one has read

---

1 For the texts/citations of Byron, I use *Lord Byron: The Complete Poetical Works*, ed. Jerome McGann, 7 vols (Oxford: Clarendon Press, 1980–93), hereafter *CPW*.

2 As Jerome Christensen has argued, Byron's literary and celebrity development consisted of the decades-long "collaborative invention of a gifted poet, a canny publisher, eager reviewers, and rapt readers." Jerome Christensen, *Lord Byron's Strength: Romantic Writing and Commercial Society* (Baltimore: Johns Hopkins University Press, 1993), xx.

3 Letter to Thomas Moore of 28 August 1813, in Lord Byron, *Byron's Letters and Journals*, ed. Leslie A. Marchand, 12 vols, vol. 3 (Cambridge: Harvard University Press, 1973–81), 101. Subsequent references to this edition will be cited as *BLJ* (3: 101). While Moore's own deployments of Orientalism in works like *Lalla Rookh* are anchored in allegories of Irish nationalism, Byron, in addition to nationalist commentary, seeks expressions of anxious otherness, that is, alterity, in the literary and geographically unmoored "Orient" he creates.

4 As Nick Mason argues, tracing the marketing practices of *Childe Harold's Pilgrimage* recasts the material factors of "advertising and literature, the commodities industry and the culture industry" within a specific moment of literary history: Byron's popular rise (439). For more on Byron's rise to fame in the context of product branding and commodified aesthetics, see Nicholas Mason, "Building Brand Byron: Early-Nineteenth-Century Advertising and the Marketing of *Childe Harold's Pilgrimage*," *MLQ: Modern Language Quarterly* 63, no. 4 (2002): 411–40.

when one has seen only one's own country."[5] This cosmopolitan "universe" also presaged the emergence of Byron's Orientalism in the Eastern Tales.[6] For example, the final canto of the *Pilgrimage* begins with the initial setting of Venice personified as a seductive woman with "spoils of nations, and the exhaustless East / Pour[ing] in her lap all gems in sparkling showers" (4.2.15–16). Venice is positioned in contradistinction to the far "East," yet a cultural exchange is still apparent. This type of cultural comparison fuels much of Byron's work after the *Pilgrimage*, as seen in the Eastern Tales and their shifting cultural repertoires.

Rather than naming the tales as already Orientalist, I assert the charged apposition between Orientalism and worldliness, i.e. cosmopolitanism, that marks Byron's character representations. This appositional relationship creates the device of Orientalist plurality as a metonym for Romantic universalism. In using "cosmopolitanism," I am referring to both the modern view of a common humanity and the long tradition of Immanuel Kant's writings in "Toward Perpetual Peace," "Idea for Universal History with a Cosmopolitan Purpose," and the *Critique of Judgment*.[7] Kant's model of cosmopolitanism also sets the terms of aesthetic taste-making and disagreement over what constitutes universal forms of literary production.[8] As Manu Chander asserts, however, Kant's model of cosmopolitanism argues for "ideals of global participation" only to a point.[9] For Byron, like his peers, this point is the exclusion of women and people of color from the same legislative and representational rights as their white male counterparts.

---

5   Translated from French, the epigraph from Fougeret de Monbron's *Le Cosmopolite* reads, "The universe is a sort of book, whose first page one has read when one has seen only one's own country. I have leafed through a great many that I have found equally bad. This inquiry has not been at all unfruitful. I hated my country. All the oddities of the different people among whom I have lived have reconciled me to it. Should I gain no other benefit from my travels than this, I will have regretted neither the pains nor the fatigues" (*CPW* 2: 3). For more on the epigraph, see Frederick Garber, *Self, Text, and Romantic Irony: The Example of Byron* (Princeton: Princeton University Press, 2014) and Joanna Wilkes, *Lord Byron and Madame de Staël: Born for Opposition* (Abingdon UK: Routledge Press, 2018).

6   See also Naji B. Ouejian, "Orientalism: The Romantics' Added Dimension; or, Edward Said Refuted," in *Romanticism in Its Modern Aspects: Review of National Literatures and World Report*, ed. Anna Paolucci and Virgil Nemoianu (Wilmington: Council on National Literatures, 1998). Ouejian writes that the "the first quarter of the nineteenth century witnessed two significant strains of Orientalism in Romantic literature ... a burst of Orientalism in prose-fiction ... [and] the second wave in the form of poetry" (41).

7   All citations from Kant's political writings are taken from the second edition of Kant's *Political Writings*, ed. H. Reiss, trans. H. B Nisbet (Cambridge: Cambridge University Press, 1991). I am thinking of Kant's argument for peaceful world interaction in "Toward Perpetual Peace" including republicanism as the state norm, a worldwide "federation of free states," and "world citizenship" as defined by "conditions of universal hospitality" (99–106). See also Adriana Craciun, "Citizens of the World: Émigrés, Romantic Cosmopolitanism, and Charlotte Smith," *Nineteenth-Century Contexts* 29, vols 2–3 (2007): 169–85.

8   Kant deems taste a type of aesthetic judgment. See Immanuel Kant, *The Critique of Judgment*, trans. James Creed Meredith (Oxford: Clarendon Press, 1973).

9   Manu Chander, *Brown Romantics: Poetry and Nationalism in the Global Nineteenth Century* (Lewisburg, PA and London: Bucknell University Press, 2017), 9.

By the time he composed *Lara*, Byron has created an ambiguously cosmopolitan persona that is predicated on a more global sense of the poetic subject. At the end of the tale, Lara is mortally wounded, and his last living gesture is to point "to the *East*" (*CPW* 2.467, emphasis mine).

After the predominantly European settings of the *Pilgrimage*, Lara's gesture confirms Byron's creation of an imagined and textualized "East" from which Byron was building his literary identity. This dying gesture serves as the culmination of Byron's provocation of settings in "the East" and raises new questions for Byron's poetics, including the role of early nineteenth-century discourses of Westernization, the link between poetic subjectivity and place, and geographical and ethnic significations as verse tale motifs.[10] In effect, these tales represent how Byron's cosmopolitanism is forged directly by his creation of an imagined "East." In order to create and populate this "East," Byron moves the hero archetype of the *Pilgrimage* into a largely invented poetic space without clear signifiers of cultural representation. As a series, the Eastern Tales also forge a poetic space peripheral to Westernized or "British" poetic conventions.

Byron's Emergent Orientalism: A Revised Cosmopolitanism

If, as Kant defines it, cosmopolitanism is "the matrix within which all original capacities of the human race may develop," what happens when this "human race" is presumed to have a European center and Eastern periphery, as Byron's Eastern Tales confirm?[11] Gerard Cohen-Vrignaud identifies a Romantic-era "radical Orientalism [...] that is invested in giving a 'contrarian' voice to marginalized or non-conforming Britons."[12] Saree Makdisi recognizes an imperial aspect of Byron's cosmopolitanism in terms of a bourgeois "self who can come and go unfettered and feel, or claim to feel, at home anywhere."[13] I argue that these tales both popularize and normalize Orientalist representations.

10   After *Lara*, Byron's two remaining Eastern tales, *The Siege of Corinth* and *Parisina*, were published anonymously in the same volume in February 1816, just before his wife left him and after the Battle of Waterloo, both which would rupture his own poetic historiography. Also, in terms of historical narratives, they lack "Eastern" or "Turkish" perspective in that they lack Turkish characters, take place in classically imagined Greece and Italy, and presage Byron's philhellenic impulse. For more on Byron's Arabic-Islamic sources, see Samar Attar's *Borrowed Imagination: The British Romantics and Their Arabic-Islamic Sources* (Lanham, MD: Lexington Books, 2014).

11   Kant, *Political Writings*, 51. In the third article of "Toward Perpetual Peace" Kant argues that "all men are entitled to present themselves in the society of others by virtue of their communal possession of the earth's surface. Since the earth is a globe, they cannot disperse over an infinite area, but must necessarily tolerate one's company" (106).

12   Gerard Cohen-Vrignaud, *Radical Orientalism: Rights, Reform, and Romanticism* (Cambridge: Cambridge University Press, 2015), 8. Cohen-Vrignaud argues that many Western writers of the Romantic era "looked East to articulate their sexual nonconformity" and in addition, represented queer or non-normative subjectivities as mouthpieces for marginalized Britons (*Radical Orientalism* 8). He concludes that "[g]rasping the Orient's lure as a representational weapon in the battles between the forces of reform and those of reaction helps us account more fully for the proliferation of exoticism in the nineteenth century and the multiplicity of ambitions it could and did encode" (9). This "multiplicity of ambitions" is a site of contested literary importance and canonicity.

13   Saree Makdisi, *Making England Western: Occidentalism, Race, and Imperial Culture* (Chicago and London: University of Chicago Press, 2014), 152.

These four Eastern Tales share literary devices and motifs that characterize a larger paradigm shift in British cultural representations. These devices and motifs include the universalized "Oriental" subject, non-British hero/anti-hero archetypes, inconsistent geographical settings, cultural generalizations, and sexual objectification.[14] These choices reflects a larger developing genre of Orientalist poetics discussed by Emily Haddad, Mohammed Sharafuddin, Saree Makdisi and others. Emily Haddad argues for the aesthetic link between nineteenth-century poetry and Orientalism, noting that "[n]ineteenth-century aesthetics constitutes the Islamic Orient in particular as a fundamentally amimetic site."[15] The lack of mimesis, I argue, creates a diffuse problem of representation across many Romantic-era works, including Byron's Eastern Tales. Fundamentally, the problem consists of literary characters and settings that lack a basis in empirical or first-hand experience. Given Byron's own travels, an experiential writing of the "East" could have been expected—the type of literature based on an increasingly direct knowledge of the "East" through travel, ethnographic reports, and studies. However, Byron's "literary orientalism," as Stephen Cheeke notes, "relied upon just such firsthand knowledge, but it was a knowledge that was carefully prepared for the reading public's consumption."[16] The tales were produced and reproduced at a rate of consumption for the reading public, and their defining features are not empirical, but aesthetic. What exact Orientalist line to take and from what sources remains an open question complicated by the runaway sales of each Eastern installment.

Byron relies less on ornamental settings, lurid plot development, or supernatural imagery than contemporary works like William Beckford's *Vathek*.[17] In terms of genre, his tales also shift in verse form and meter, reshaping the romance form and Spenserian stanzas of *Childe Harold's Pilgrimage* into octosyllabic and heroic couplets as well as complete versus fragment forms. Byron pays close attention to character development and poetic voice, as well as the representations of anxious subjectivities. Oftentimes, these representations are deployed along the lines of sex and gender, whereas other times, Byron renders his characters interchangeable without clear individuation.[18] These choices reflect a long line of Anglophone writers writing during

---

14   Emily Haddad writes at length on the bridge between nineteenth-century poetry and Orientalism in *Orientalist Poetics: The Islamic Middle East in Nineteenth-Century English and French Poetry* (Aldershot: Ashgate, 2001). She elucidates how nineteenth-century poetry uses Orientalist tropes in order to create "an alternative aesthetic space in which poems play out a variety of responses to both contemporary and past trends in poetry" (2).

15   Haddad, *Orientalist Poetics*, 3.

16   Stephen Cheeke, *Byron and Place: History, Translation, Nostalgia* (Basingstoke: Palgrave Macmillan, 2003), 13.

17   Like Shelley, William Beckford, and Robert Southey, Byron was heavily influenced by Sir William Jones's foundational Orientalist scholarship.

18   Scholars including Makdisi and Cohen-Vrignaud locate desire as integral to the character representations in the tales. In terms of Byron's representations of gender, his women characters are described inconsistently, disparately, and diffusely, as Shahidha Bari notes in "Listening for Leila: The Re-direction of Desire in Byron's *The Giaour*," *European Romantic Review*, 24, no. 6 (2013)): 699–721.

an era of British Orientalism's popular rise. In turn, the tales' marketability and popular success legitimate the practice of ambiguous cultural representation as part of Romantic poetics.[19]

With their distant settings oriented toward "the East," the tales experiment with drawing and creating literary worlds along hemispheric and/or geographical lines. Scholars including Stephen Cheeke, Katarina Gephardt, Saree Makdisi, Diego Saglia, Andrew Warren, and others, have written on Byron's geographical and cultural poetics.[20] As Makdisi argues, "the space that would eventually come to be established as the Occident had to be Occidentalized—that England, among other sites, had to be made Western."[21] This Westernization occurred, in literature, via poetic form and content shifts such as Byron's choice of traditional and newer verse forms, cultural stereotypes, and generalizations coded as "Eastern" or "Oriental" expression. The Romantic period's turn to imagination and expression affords the formative topoi from which Byron was able not only to gain celebrity status in Britain, Europe, and the Americas but also to market his vision without the expectation of verisimilitude or realistic representations. Without this expectation, Byron creates new poetic spaces and subjects lacking clear geographical or cultural boundaries.

Byron's turn to the "East" after the *Pilgrimage* reflects an important juncture of Byron coming to terms with his new literary celebrity, what Jerome McGann calls Byron's "careerist calculation."[22] In addition to being careerist opportunities and "Orientalist" miscellany, the tales also reflect Byron's self-reflexive anxieties in contributing to an Anglophone poetic tradition that he wanted to opt in and out of freely. This notion of choice, choosing to participate or not in traditional forms, also registers Byron's shift in literary aesthetics to less familiar and newer forms of cultural production and commodification. The tales, in effect, reinforce

See also, Caroline Franklin, "Some samples of the finest Orientalism': Byronic Philhellenism and proto-Zionism at the time of the Congress of Vienna," in *Romanticism and Colonialism: Writing and Empire 1780–1830*, ed. Tim Fulford and Peter J. Kitson (New York: Cambridge University Press, 1998), 229.

19   In terms of ethnic representation, *The Giaour*'s heroine, Leila, is Circassian. In *The Bride*, Zuleika is Turkish, along with the other protagonists, Selim and Giaffir. In *The Corsair*, the Aegean pirate hero, Conrad, is joined by a new heroine, Gulnare. Described as "The Haram queen—but still the slave of Seyd," Gulnare assassinates the Turkish pasha Seyd after joining forces with Conrad (*CPW* 3: 2.224). In the *Corsair*'s supposed "sequel," *Lara*, Gulnare has been transplanted by Lara's faithful page, Kaled, who has ambiguous gender, ethnicity, and religious signification and is given no dialogue in the work.

20   See Stephen Cheeke, *Byron and Place: History, Translation, Nostalgia* (Basingstoke: Palgrave Macmillan, 2003); Katarina Gephardt, "The Occidentalist Costume: Lord Byron and Travelers' Perspectives on Eastern Europe," in *The Idea of Europe in British Travel Narratives, 1789–1914* (Abingdon: Routledge University Press, 2014); Makdisi, *Making England Western*; Diego Saglia, "Locating Byron: Languages, Voices, and Displaced Utterances," *Philological Quarterly* 86, no. 4 (Fall 2007): 393–414; and Andrew Warren, *The Orient and the Young Romantics* (Cambridge: Cambridge University Press, 2014).

21   Makdisi, *Making England Western*, xiii.

22   Jerome J. McGann, *Byron and Romanticism*, ed. James Soderholm (Cambridge and New York: Cambridge University Press, 2002), 37; Jerome J. McGann, "Byron, mobility, and the poetics of historical ventriloquism," *Romanticism Past and Present* 9, no. 1 (1985): 67–82, doi: 10.1080/08905498 508583230.

a defamiliarized poetic perspective oriented towards newly foreign subjects and content. The commodification of "Byron" as a poetic brand happened throughout Byron's career. Yet after the runaway success of the *Pilgrimage*, the subsequent moment of aesthetic invention, the Tales, have been overlooked by critics largely for their difficulty to read and situate in Byron's larger oeuvre.

While *Childe Harold's Pilgrimage* ends with Harold's point of view fully discarded for Byron's own, the Eastern Tales shift the characters and settings to far-flung settings that never are reintegrated fully into Byron's position as poet. These representations mark a clear shift in Byron's aesthetics, propelling his poetic form and content towards less mimetic modes.[23] This shift yields Byron the opportunity to create and self-create, to avoid the task of realistic representations, and to aestheticize his own poetic subjectivity.[24]

Reading the Tales

The first of these tales to be published, *The Giaour: A Fragment of a Turkish Tale*, announced Byron's claiming of the "East" as a part of the cosmopolitan realm ushered in by the *Pilgrimage*. Byron writes in the Advertisement, "The tale which these disjointed fragments present, is founded upon circumstances now less common in the East than formerly" (*CPW* 3: 39).[25] The tale resists a coherent reading via its "fragment" form and use of multiple narrators, including the eponymous Giaour.[26] Contemporary reviews of the poem picked up on these questions of form, genre, and fragmentation, but they did not attend to the heterogeneity of the geographical and ethnic significations.[27] To

---

23   By the *Pilgrimage*'s final canto, published in April 1818, Harold's point of view has been discarded, and Byron writes in a letter to John Hobhouse that he [has or had] "become weary of drawing a line which every one seemed not to perceive: like the Chinese in Goldsmith's *Citizen of the World*, whom nobody would believe to be a Chinese, it was in vain that I asserted, and imagined, that I had drawn a distinction between the author and the pilgrim; and the very anxiety to preserve this difference, and disappointment at finding it unavailing, so far crushed my efforts in the composition, that I determined to abandon it altogether" (*CPW* 2: 122).

24   Edward Said assesses these types of "pilgrimage" literatures in *Orientalism* to be fundamental to Orientalist poetics. Said writes of the Romantic pilgrimage, "From one end of the nineteenth century to the other—after Napoleon, that is—the Orient was a place of pilgrimage, and every major work belonging to a genuine if not always to an academic Orientalism took its form, style, and intention from the idea of pilgrimage there. In this idea as in so many of the other forms of Oriental writing we have been discussing, the Romantic notion of restorative reconstruction ([M. H. Abrams's] natural supernaturalism) is the principal source." Edward Said, *Orientalism* (New York: Vintage, 1979), 168.

25   The work's epigraph and prefatory "Advertisement" introduce the tale within a traditionary non-Eastern frame. The epigraph comes from Thomas Moore's *Irish Melodies* and the "Advertisement" famously invokes the tomb of ancient Athenian democrat, Themistocles, asking "When shall such hero live again?" (6).

26   Written in late 1812, *The Giaour* is not only fragmented but also filled with plot holes and disordered chronology, partially due to Byron continually adding lines of different lengths to the work from an initial 344 to a final 1,334 lines by the seventh edition (*BLJ* 3: 100). The tale is written predominantly in tetrameter verse and rhyming couplets.

27   For example, *The British Review* called *The Giaour* a "poetical anatomy" with a "mincing, comminuting, and subdividing method" (136, 134). *The British Review* 5 (October 1813).

do so was to overlook the potent forces of literary worldmaking and, "empire building" at play within each new "fragment" added to the "snake of a poem" (*BLJ* 3: 100).[28] Marilyn Butler notes that critics should take the tales' "geographical significations" at "face value" since for Byron and his contemporary "materialist poets ... the place of a poem's setting means what it says, and the time is always in some sense the present."[29] If she is correct, one must attend to the work's geographies and inconsistent cultural significations. This attention offers a key to understanding not only Byron's creation of a textualized East, but also an acknowledgment of the messiness of empire embedded in Byron's early-career Eastern representations.

The tale's "present" place and time involves the "Giaour," a Christian-born Venetian and infidel who fights against the Turkish emir Hassan for the love of a young Circassian woman, Leila.[30] Eventually Leila is drowned by Hassan upon his discovery of her affair with the Giaour.[31] The opening speaker laments Greece's lost classicism, under Turkish rule at the time, in a continuation of the antiquity trope from the *Pilgrimage*. In a continuation of his aestheticization of the "East," Byron describes Port Leone's shore as awash in "the lovely light / That best becomes an Eastern night" (177–9). Amid this scene, an anonymous Turkish fisherman arrives at Port Leone and sees the Giaour, riding by with "Christian crest and haughty mien" (256). These lines immediately position the identifiable heroism away from the Venetian Giaour, and the reader is transported to Byron's "boundless East" (452).

---

28   Toni Morrison writes, "Canon building is empire building. Canon defense is national defense. Canon debate, whatever the terrain, nature, and range (of criticism, of history, of the history of knowledge, of the definition of language, the universality of aesthetic principles, the sociology of art, the humanistic imagination), is the clash of cultures. And all of the interests are vested." Toni Morrison, "Unspeakable Things Unspoken: The Afro-American Presence in American Literature" (The Tanner Lectures on Human Values, The University of Michigan, Ann Arbor, 1988), 132.
29   Marilyn Butler, "The Orientalism of Byron's *Giaour*," in *Byron and the Limits of Fiction*, ed. Bernard Beatty and Vincent Newey (Liverpool: Rowman & Littlefield, 1988), 78–96.
30   "Giaour" is used today as a derogatory term (Turkish: "Gâvur"), similar to the Arabic word "Kafir," both terms meaning a non-believer.
31   Byron cites William Beckford's villain in *Vathek* as a source for his "Giaour" (*CPW* 3: 415). Beckford's influence includes Byron's usage of the word "giaour." Byron began *The Giaour* in September 1812, the month he wrote the "Addition to the Preface" for the fourth edition of the *Pilgrimage*. See Lord Byron, *CPW* 2: 269; 3: 413. *Vathek* inspired a number of other Orientalist enterprises, including the Middle Eastern setting of Southey's *Thalaba the Destroyer* (1801), Thomas Moore's *Lalla-Rookh* (1817), and John Keats's underworld setting in *Endymion* (1818), as well as Edgar Allan Poe's "Tamerlane" and "Landor's Cottage." Similar in genre to *The Giaour*, Clare A. Simmons notes how Robert Southey's combination of poetic text and notes in *Thalaba the Destroyer* is the "first major instance of the genre" (85). In addition to being an Orientalist "fragment" inspired by Samuel Rogers's fragment, *Voyage of Columbus*, *The Giaour*'s genre can [be] classified as "scholarly annotated poetry" and frame narrative poem (Ruth Knezevich, "The Empire of the Page: Footnotes in Byron's *The Giaour*," *Essays in Romanticism* 24, no. 1 [2017]: 35). Additionally, it is inspired by the "general form of the modern Greek ballads about Euphrosyne which B[yron] had heard when he was in the Near East" (*CPW* 3: 415). Knezevich 35–52; Clare A. Simmons, "'Useful and Wasteful Both': Southey's *Thalaba the Destroyer* and the Function of Annotation in the Romantic Oriental Poem," *Genre: Forms of Discourse and Culture* 27, nos 1–2 (1994): 83–104.

This space, as Byron describes, is one of the "Edens of the eastern wave" (15)—water imagery that invokes the story of Leila's drowning.[32]

After the Giaour has ridden by on a steed, Byron introduces Leila for the first time, yet she is neither named nor given dialogue.[33] Leila's layered identity as Turkish woman, Muslim, slave, and sexualized object is obfuscated by her lack of dialogue and point of view throughout the work. Furthermore, her symbolism of ideal womanhood reinforces normative conceptions of gender and heteronormative relationships. Thus, she occupies the space of Spivak's subaltern, "caught between tradition and modernization."[34] This liminality, as Shahidha Bari notes, makes Leila "the void around which the entire narrative is generated."[35] The speaker ponders if Leila is a "soulless toy for tyrant's lust?" and then describes her "fair cheek's unfading hue" as well as "[h]er hair in hyacinthine flow" and how "midst her handmaids in the hall / She stood superior to them all" (490–9). Leila's "fair" Circassian skin and "superior" status constitute her racialized whiteness, yet she remains otherwise unrepresented in terms of physical description, race, and ethnicity. Leila's representation reinforces the disjointed nature of the work and opens up a gendered space of imagined alterity for Byron's growing audience.

The opacity of the representation of Leila is not singular. Byron represents the Giaour and Hassan sparingly in terms of physical description, often likening them in terms of appearance.[36] Once the battle between Hassan and the Giaour commences, Byron brings in Turkish references—"arquebuss," "ataghan," "pasha," "Tartar," and "Chiaus" (522, 530, 549, 571)—verbiage that adds a type of Orientalist firsthand knowledge, to the imaginative setting. In discussing the postmodern world we inhabit, Said famously argues that "standardization and cultural stereotyping have intensified the hold of the nineteenth-century academic and imaginative demonology of 'the mysterious Orient'" (26). Said distinguishes between "academic," "scholarly," and "imaginative" Orientalism throughout his works, yet this distinction does not hold when applied to Byron's tales. Byron's unsystematic practice of cultural references creates a habitually East-facing perspective without clear center or periphery. In *The Giaour* this results in both imaginative and scholarly deployments of Orientalism.

---

32   In terms of ethnographic influence, Byron's work invokes the Turkish oral tradition, as the story of Leila's drowning at the hands of Hassan is a common folk tale derived from the drowning of several women by Ottoman Albanian ruler, Ali Pasha Tepelena, whom Byron famously met in 1809.

33   Via Hassan's implied point of view, Byron writes of Hassan's drowning of Leila, how he "watch'd as it [her bundled body] sank" into the "tide" where "all its hidden secrets sleep, / Known but to Genii of the deep" (376, 383, 384–5). This scene is a dialogue between another anonymous fisherman and Hassan / "Emir" (1.357).

34   Gayatri Chakravorty Spivak, "Can the Subaltern Speak?" in *Colonial Discourse and Post-colonial Theory: A Reader*, ed. Patrick Williams and Laura Chrisman (New York, Sydney: Harvester Wheatsheaf, 1993), 66–111.

35   Bari, 710.

36   The Giaour is described as having "dark hair" and "pale brow" (894–5), but he lacks the racialized whiteness of Leila.

Nowhere does Byron more conspicuously veer away from Said's ontology than in this climactic battle between Hassan and the Giaour. Rather than deploying a binary framing of self/other or East/West, the speaker extols sympathy on Hassan while rebuking the Giaour. The Giaour is condemned by the speaker for being "array'd in Arnaut garb, / Apostate from his own vile faith, / [that] shall not save him from the death" (615–17). The reference to the Giaour's cultural appropriation and apostasy interrogates the heroism of both the Giaour and Hassan, culminating in their mirroring at battle scene's end. The Giaour bends over "Fall'n Hassan," "that foe with brow / As dark as his that bled below—" (669, 673–4). This mirroring compresses Byron's hero trope into the intersubjective perspective of the Giaour and Hassan. The Giaour speaks for the first time in the next passage, responding, "Yes, Leila sleeps beneath the wave, / But his [Hassan] shall be a redder grave … He call'd the Prophet, but his power / Was vain against the vengeful Giaour" (675–80). The Giaour's illeism reflects not only narcissism but the artifice of his representation, further evidenced by the convenient end-rhyme. This illeism implies external observation, the construct-edness of the Orientalist imaginary, and Byron's experimentation with new ways of describing the world and his expanded poetic subjectivity.

After the battle scene, the disjointedness of the work is increasingly apparent in the continuous shifting of narrative perspectives. Byron turns to the perspective of an unnamed Turkish man who reflects on the contrasting fates of the Giaour and Hassan. Next, he reverts back to the initial fisherman who saw the Giaour chasing Hassan by horse (723–86).[37] This fisherman converses with a monk in the abbey where the Giaour has become a religious recluse and "lone Caloyer" (787). The Giaour has become a fallen hero, unable to live in society, who steadfastly "broods within his cell alone, / His faith and race alike unknown" (806–7). The tale's anonymous speaker, in a tone of imperial anxiety, ponders, "Yet seems he not of Othman race, But only Christian in his face" (810–11). The Giaour has acquired a religious and racial obscurity beyond the limits of the Orientalist frame and does not fit within the purview of the racialized identities scaffolded by Byron.

Instead, the Giaour becomes a spectral presence and persistently "mutters" in his cell of Leila (822), raving of his past to the empty cell walls. As a haunted figure, the Giaour internalizes the violence and murders of Leila and Hassan. He seeks relief in "hate":

> If solitude succeed to grief,
> Release from pain is slight relief;

---

37   Matthew J. A. Green writes that "[w]ith its provisions of fragmentary narratives focalized through multiple perspectives, *The Giaour* serves to demonstrate not only the power of the frame but also [its] flexibility [and its ability] to entertain radically opposed framing procedures without suspending ethical judgments," in "'That lifeless thing the living fear'; Freedom, Community, and the Gothic Body in *The Giaour*," *Byron and the Politics of Freedom and Terror*, ed. Matthew J. A. Green and Piya Pal-Lapinski (Basingstoke: Palgrave, 1988), 15–32 (30).

[...]
The heart once left thus desolate
Must fly at last for ease—to hate. (937–40)

Following this internal meditation, the Giaour, in a dramatic monologue expressed to the abbot, confesses his culpability for Leila's death. Contrasting with the abbot's "generous tear," the Giaour's "glazing eye" evokes the prophet-seer figure in Coleridge's *The Rime of the Ancient Mariner* and Beckford's eponymous character in *Vathek* (1323). The Giaour's "glazing eye" registers a type of paralysis or self-reflexive condemnation. Rather than responding or absolving him of sin, the abbot remains silent. Like the silence of Leila and Hassan's mother, the silence of the abbot reifies the Giaour's solipsism.[38]

This moment of confession is the resolution for the narrative, but the "tale" ends, in the words of the Giaour, "broken" (1333). In the final footnote to the poem, Byron qualifies the scholarly and historical credibility of the work. This footnote reveals not only Byron's self-fashioning of his cultural repertoire but his awareness of the work's questionable "correctness" and "originality." Byron writes:

> The circumstance to which the above story relates was not very uncommon in Turkey ... . The story in the text is one told of a young Venetian many years ago, and now nearly forgotten. I heard it by accident recited by one of the coffee-house story-tellers who abound in the Levant, and sing or recite their narratives ... . I regret that my memory has retained so few fragments of the original ... . For the contents of some of the notes I am indebted partly to D'Herbelot, and partly to that most Eastern, and, as Mr. Weber justly entitles it, "sublime tale," [Beckford's] the "Caliph Vathek." ... for correctness of costume, beauty of description, and power of imagination, it far surpasses all European imitations; and bears such marks of originality, that those who have visited the East will find some difficulty in believing it to be more than a translation. (*CPW* 3: 422–3)[39]

The prolepsis of this footnote recalls the preface, where Byron stakes a claim for the intended authenticity of his tale. As one of many "European imitations" that still "bears such marks of originality," Byron wrote *The Giaour* in the service of "originality" more than "correctness of costume" or credibility. By work's end,

---

38   Like Leila, Hassan's mother is left without dialogue in the work, completely silent in the passage where she is told by an anonymous Tartar messenger of her son, Hassan's, murder at the hands of the Giaour (*CPW* 3: 689–722).
39   Cf. Byron's revised yet unpublished footnote referring to Lord Sligo (*CPW* 3: 423–4).

Hassan, Leila, and their culturally ambiguous representations have been bookended by the self-referential "tale" of the Giaour.[40]

Just eight months after the initial publication of *The Giaour*, *The Bride of Abydos* was published in December 1813.[41] In a letter to Thomas Moore a month earlier, Byron apologizes for his lack of correspondence and shares with Moore that he will be sending along another work soon, *The Bride of Abydos*, which was written "for the sake of the *employment*" (*BLJ* 3: 184).[42] The fact that Byron seeks out Moore's approval and feedback on his next Eastern tale shows a more apprehensive and calculated approach than in *The Giaour*, which his publisher John Murray published "at his own risk" (*BLJ* 3: 59). Byron also asserts that *The Bride* is "another Turkish story" but "*not* a Fragment" (*BLJ* 3: 184; emphasis added). In indicating that the tale is not a fragment like *The Giaour*, Byron's shift in form and aestheticization of a more coherent subjectivity are apparent. Byron is careful to note that *The Bride* "does not trench upon your [Moore's] kingdom in the least, and, if it did, you would soon reduce me to my proper boundaries" (*BLJ* 3: 184). In "kingdom" Byron is referring to Moore's own Orientalist romance, *Lalla Rookh*, which Moore conceived of writing a year earlier.

Byron's more measured approach to this tale can be seen in his attention to the work's diction and syntax. At the beginning of November, Byron wrote to Murray, "Pray attend to the *corrections* they are slight but *important* and remember the *Bride*" (*BLJ* 3:156). On 13 November, after a series of corrections and edits, Byron specifically asked Murray to revise lines 1073–4—a speech by Zuleika, the heroine of the *Bride*:

> (the only one of *hers* [speech] in that Canto)—
> it is now thus—
>   "And curse—if I could curse—the day"
> it must be
>   "And mourn—I dare not curse—the day" (*BLJ* 3.163)[43]

---

40   Matthew J. A. Green writes that "[c]ertainly the world we live in is vulnerable and precarious, but one of the key lessons to be gleaned from *The Giaour* is that, as Badiou notes elsewhere, if we want to move to 'a single world of human subjects,' we need to avoid fixation on topics such as integration and cultural difference: 'the single world is precisely the place where an unlimited set of differences exist'" (30).

41   Byron wrote *The Bride* either in a purported four nights or one week alongside his editing and finishing of *The Giaour* (*BLJ* 3: 156).

42   The sentence continues, "—to wring my thoughts from reality, and take refuge in 'imaginings,' however 'horrible'" (*BLJ* 3: 184). It is also telling that Byron seeks validation from Moore, an Irish national poet who is unaffiliated with the Lake School.

43   Later in the letter, Byron also asked that "in the last M.S. lines sent—instead of 'living heart' correct to 'quivering heart' it is in line 9th of the M.S. passage" (3.163). Byron sent over thirty letters of correction and revision to his publisher, John Murray, in the month leading up to the 2 December 1813 publication of the *Bride*.

This change in Zuleika's dialogue from "curse" to "mourn" and "could curse" to "dare not curse" tempers her ire and reinforces her passive characterization and idealized "purity" (*BLJ* 3: 199).[44] While in *The Giaour* Leila remains silent within the text and her characterization is simplistic, Zuleika's dialogue and action in the *Bride* do play a role in the plot's resolution. The resolution also offers narrative closure after the disjointedness of *The Giaour*.

As the tales progress, the forms and motifs Byron chooses to continue or adapt remain unpredictable and open to interpretation. While Byron turns from fragment to complete "story" in the *Bride,* he maintains varying tetrameter and octosyllabic couplets, continuing with *The Giaour*'s meter. Byron begins the work with an landscape of culturally diffuse images, writing of "cypress and myrtle" "cedar and vine," and "gardens of Gúl" where "the flowers ever blossom, the beams ever shine" (1–13).[45] This imagery heralds the Pasha Giaffir's introduction in the next stanza.

Viewed through the omniscient narrator's point of view, Giaffir is placed as object among the Orientalist accoutrements and characters that surround him. Byron writes,

> Old Giaffir sate in his Divan,
> Deep thought was in his aged eye;
> And though the face of Mussulman
> Not oft betrays to standers by
> The mind within, well skill'd to hide
> All but unconquerable pride,
> His pensive cheek and pondering brow
> Did more than he was wont avow. (1. 24–31)

At first wordless, Giaffir is depicted as sitting in a "Divan," with single "aged eye" and "the face of Mussulman" with a "Nubian" servant at his behest (1.35). These aestheticized signifiers create a character objectified through association with "Oriental" objects.

In the next canto, the "Turkish" setting is re-invoked through an imagined setting of the Dardanelles strait/the "Helle" (2.1). Byron's aestheticization of subjectivity recurs through Selim's impassioned reveal to Zuleika. Selim throws off his "robe of pride" and "high-crown'd turban" in a Byronic flourish, and confesses to Zuleika,

> I said I was not what I seemed—
> And now thou see'st my words were true;

---

44   Byron writes to his friend Dr. Clark on his intention in writing *The Bride of Abydos:* "I also wished to try my hand on a female character in Zuleika—& have endeavoured as far as ye. grossness of our masculine ideas will allow—to preserve her *purity* without impairing the ardour of the attachment" (*BLJ* 3: 199; emphasis added).

45   *CPW* 3: 1.1–13. All *Bride* quotations hereafter will be cited with canto and line number. "Gúl" is the Persian word for "rose."

I have a tale thou hast not dreamed,
If sooth—its truth must others rue. (2.151–4)

After his circuitous invocation, Selim confesses, "Zuleika! I am not thy brother!"
(2.163–4). Having learned of his true identity from Giaffir's servant, Haroun, Selim's
mistreatment by Giaffir now makes sense to him.[46] Zuleika responds, "God! Am I
left alone on earth?— / To mourn—I dare not curse—the day / That saw my solitary
birth!" (2.166–8). Here, her revised speech registers differently from Byron's initial
line in his letter to Murray: "And curse—if I could curse—the day" (*BLJ* 3.163). This
edit from "curse" to "mourn" hedges Zuleika's agency. Zuleika's diminished agency
extends into the next scene where she stands "mute and motionless," immobilized as
a "statue of distress," and dies of sorrow (2.491–2).

Byron, on completing the work, deems *The Bride of Abydos*, "horrible enough,"
and in effect, a poetic disappointment (*BLJ* 3: 160). Byron attempts to set and reset
the terms of his developing poetics through new and unfinished aesthetic spaces
and subjects. In doing so, he creates new literary worlds but also tests the limits of
literariness and literary taste. His increasingly obscure cosmopolitan realm offers a
growing number of cultural representations and heroic characters that trouble the
boundaries between what it means to be both part of and apart from a space of
geographical, familial, and national identity. Rather than reinforcing the imagined
"East" and its attendant cultural heterogeneity as a trope *par excellence*, Byron's next
two Eastern Tales, *The Corsair* and *Lara*, default, instead, to self-reflexive representations of Byron's own subjectivity.[47]

Conrad and Lara: The Shifting Coordinates of Byron's Cosmopolitan "East"

After selling all 10,000 copies on its first day of sale, the next of the Eastern Tales, *The
Corsair* (1814), was another boon for Byron's literary success. In terms of its inception,
Byron's anxieties, however, are explicit. For example, Byron's prefatory letter to
Thomas Moore at the beginning of *The Corsair* deems the tale "the last production
with which I shall trespass on public patience, and your indulgence, for some years;
and I own that I feel anxious to avail myself of this latest and only opportunity"
(*CPW* 3: 148). Byron then raises the notion of national identity and his and Moore's
shared poetic alliance. He asserts that

> While *Ireland* ranks you [Moore] amongst the foremost of her patriots
> – while you stand alone the first of her bards in her estimation, and

---

46   Selim's father is Abdallah, Giaffir's brother, whom Giaffir murdered. Selim does not understand
exactly what "strife to rancour grew" in this Cain and Abel parable that Byron recreates between
Giaffir and Abdallah (2.213).
47   This self-reflexive subjectivity mirrors the Byronic hero found at the end of *Childe Harold's
Pilgrimage*. As Byron notes in *The Corsair*'s opening letter to Thomas Moore, "May I add a few words
on a subject on which all men are supposed to be fluent, and none agreeable?—Self" (*CPW* 3: 149).

Britain repeats and ratifies the decree – permit one, whose only regret, since our first acquaintance, has been the years he had lost before it commenced, to add the humble, but sincere suffrage of friendship, to the voice of more than one *nation*. (*CPW* 3: 148; emphasis added)

This "suffrage" of transnational literary alliance is formed in part, through their shared projection of "the East" (*CPW* 3: 150). Referring to *Lalla Rookh*, Byron flatters Moore's current "composition of a poem whose scene will be laid in the East" and notes how in *The Corsair*, he will use "the good old and now neglected heroic couplet" (3: 150). In terms of aesthetic invention, Byron is thinking not only in terms of setting, but also form and verse. Byron shifts from octosyllabic couplets in *The Bride of Abydos* to classical form and meter—narrative epic and heroic couplets—in *The Corsair* and *Lara*.

Byron's poetic development in these tales is also a revelation of his own psyche. Byron ends the dedication by both defending and criticizing his previous cast of heroes, deeming the Giaour immoral, Childe Harold "a very repulsive personage" and the upcoming corsair a possible "gloomy vanity of 'drawing from self'" (*CPW* 3: 150). This "drawing" reflects Byron's self-fashioning and act of poetic historiography. As Paul Hamilton notes, "For a time, Byron's poetry ran two histories alongside each other. The first history, moving towards a conclusion, told the story of individualism fated to run out of a distinctive idiolect. The second drew in his 'land's language' to make poetic achievement the epiphenomenon of a more Shakespearean (or Walter Scott-like) articulation of all the different registers of English."[48] Byron continues to create, revise, and redact his poetic history with each of these tales. These quasi-historical and semi-autobiographical impulses, I argue, fundamentally undergird Byron's production of *The Corsair* and *Lara* differently from the previous two tales.

The Byronic hero in *The Corsair* is Conrad, an isolated man who, like Selim in *The Bride*, is a contested hero. Unlike Selim, however, Conrad is an Aegean pirate with no clear nationality or religion, making him an "outsider" in his illegibility as a recognized subject of any nation-state.

While the stereotype posed by the tale is initially clear—a battle between the Western liberal and "Oriental" despot—Conrad's haunted conscience and perpetual bafflement with his own heroism thwart the straightforwardness of this stereotype.[49] Byron describes Conrad as "that man of loneliness and mystery,"

---

48   Paul Hamilton, "Byron, Clare, and Poetic Historiography," in *Rethinking British Romantic History, 1770–1845*, ed. Porscha Fermanis and John Regan (Oxford: Oxford University Press, 2014), 227. This dual history also reflects a "fundamental ambivalence" in the word "history" as "both experimental data and a mode of narrative," as Michael O'Neill argues in "Byron and the Aesthetics of History and Culture," in *Rethinking British Romantic History*, 207–8.

49   Mohammed Sharafuddin explains that Conrad "triumphs over him [Seyd] by assassination. Admittedly, he does not strike the blow, but he benefits from it, and he is responsible for it in that it was his action which puts Gulnare, the assassin, on his side. The fact that this action was an act of

and "Stranger!" (1.173, 243). Conrad is described physically as having "swarthy cheek with sallower hue" and, like the Giaour, is masculine and heroic but with ineffable features and "mien" (1.207). Byron writes, "His features' deepening lines and varying hue / At times attracted, yet perplexed the view, / As if within that murkiness of mind / Worked feelings fearful, and yet undefined" (1.209–12). In effect, the most consistent motif in Conrad's representation is his guilty conscience. Recursively thwarted by his conscience and "undefined" feelings, Conrad evidences the mirroring between Byron's personal anxieties and his literary characters. This mirroring is an example of Byron's projection of his poetic "mien" onto multiple personae of illegible provenance, creed, sexual orientation, race/ethnicity, and national ties.[50]

The Corsair's main characters—Conrad, Seyd, and Gulnare—populate an imagined universe left open to Byron's experimentation with poetic form and content, yet this universe is less explicitly "Eastern" than in the previous tales. Byron refers to the "East" only once in the work, when Gulnare urges Conrad to assassinate Seyd: "Oh! could'st thou prove my truth, thou would'st not start, / Nor fear the fire that lights an Eastern heart" (3.352–3). This "Eastern" stereotype blunts the agency Byron gives to Gulnare. However, this moment also marks a shift from previous representations of women, including Leila and Zuleika. Gulnare is given the role of hero and assassin, and Conrad is accessory to Gulnare's heroic act of killing their "oppressor" Seyd (3.357). By raising a woman, Gulnare, to the status of Byronic victor when she assassinates Seyd, Byron recasts female heroism as central to the question of political borders and their allegiances.[51] Instead of resolution for Gulnare or Conrad, the tale ends with the Corsair's disappearance and "death yet dubious" (3.694). In moving from Conrad's inexorable guilt in *The Corsair* to the tormented and most obscure protagonist in *Lara*, Byron realizes a Westernized cosmopolitan myth of the poetic subject delinked from clear historical or cultural context.[52]

---

liberal generosity (protectiveness towards women) only serves to entangle the web of good and evil more thoroughly." Mohammed Sharafuddin, *Islam and Romantic Orientalism: Literary Encounters with the Orient* (London; New York: Tauris, 1994), 259.

50   Conrad's attraction to Gonsalvo is a pivotal moment of queer evocation (1.153).

51   Note Conrad's passive response to Gulnare's power, as well as the relationship between Conrad and the young sailor, Gonsalvo. Peter Cochran argues that "Gulnare is the archetype for the heroines of *Don Juan* ... The strange passivity which we see in Conrad, as Gulnare persuades him to be rescued, is transmuted into the passivity of Juan before the predatory instincts of heroine after heroine" (8). See Peter Cochran, "Byron's 'Turkish Tales': An Introduction," *Newstead Abbey Byron Society*, http://www.newsteadabbeybyronsociety.org/works/downloads/turk_intro.pdf.

52   Thomas Peacock's *Essay on Fashionable Literature* (1818), which Byron's tales presage, can help us rethink the relationship between high Romanticism and Orientalism by virtue of Byron's heroic ideal. Paul Hamilton argues that "ascriptions of inferiority to the genre of popular Romanticism just beg the critical question for Peacock. Yet Peacock only highlights the political fear of the higher class of radicals that enfranchisement doesn't merely add to the numbers of the cultured classes, but rather takes them down. The new solidarity removes the very possibility of that finely tuned, imaginatively sympathetic gesture which had agitated in its radical cause." *Rethinking British Romantic History*, 227.

By the time *Lara* was published, Byron's name was culturally codified and commodified in Britain.[53] "Byromania," as Lady Byron called it, also occurred during a related moment of escalation—increased cultural representations of the "other," oftentimes the "Oriental" subject.[54] As part of this escalation, Byron's poetic subjectivity and the creation of a literary "East" are fused together. This fusing situates Byron's popular rise within a specific moment of Orientalist invention. Inventions like these—Byron's heterogeneous cultural imaginaries with obscurely "Eastern" settings—reflect larger cultural discourses of not only British cosmopolitanism but actual colonial and imperial conquest.

Lara also culminates Byron's early-career poetic experimentation with and intertwining of cosmopolitan and Orientalist practice. While Byron notes in *Lara*'s "Advertisement" that it might be seen as a "sequel" to *The Corsair* (*CPW* 3: 214), the narratives do not cohere into a unified storyline.

In addition, the setting of Lara moves beyond any notion of preconceived "East" and to an imagined world of persistently obscure time and setting without clear geographical or ethnic signifiers. Unlike the previous heroes, however, Lara is "home" and no longer voyaging across the imaginary "Orient." The protagonist has no travelogue or non-native narrative of experience for the reader to envisage. What the reader is given is Lara's immediate provincial past. Byron wrote to publisher John Murray on 24 July 1814 that Lara's "name only is Spanish—the country is not Spain but the Moon" (*BLJ* 4: 146).[55] This equivocation manifests in another array of characters and representations of ambiguous or unknown gender, religion, and ethnicity affiliations.

Rather than starting with a clear Eastern setting or invoking classical antiquity as in the prior tales, *Lara* begins by describing the eponymous protagonist's inherited property. Byron describes a provincial scene with serfs as "gay retainers" "[w]ith tongues all loudness, and with eyes all mirth" (1.1–10).[56] In this environment, Lara is famously described as "self-exiled chieftain" and "Lord of himself;—that heritage of woe" (1.4, 14). This geographically and ethnically ambiguous "heritage of woe" reflects a persona of world weariness and resistant heroism. It also reflects Byron's overexpansion of poetic subjectivity to the point of alterity beyond geographical borders.

In part, Lara's identity depends on his obscurity. In one scene, Lara walks through his halls alone at night, a phantom-like figure who does not interact with his environment. Lara's terrifying "aspect" emanates "a vital scorn of all: / As if the

---

53   *Lara* was anonymously published in 1814, between the publication of the second and third cantos of *Childe Harold's Pilgrimage*.

54   Byron's "Oriental" subject exists, as Andrew Warren notes, within "a kind of Freudian Other Scene where memory and narcissistic projection are woven into narrative" (96). Andrew Warren, *The Orient and the Young Romantics* (Cambridge: Cambridge University Press, 2014), 96.

55   As noted by critics including Diego Saglia, the work's setting may evoke Spain, but it is never stated in the work. Diego Saglia, "Locating Byron: Languages, Voices, and Displaced Utterances," *Philological Quarterly* 86, no. 4 (Fall 2007): 400–1.

56   *CPW* 3. All *Lara* quotations hereafter will be cited with canto and line number.

worst had fall'n which could befall / He stood a stranger in this breathing world" (1.313–15). As stranger and "thing of dark imaginings" whose "madness was not of the head, but heart," Lara's representation displaces anxieties of alterity onto the rhetoric of "madness" and Lara's "mental net" (1.317, 358, 381). By tale's end, Lara has been mortally wounded and his faithful page, the gender-fluid and silent Kaled, cares mutely for his limp body. In Lara's death scene, Lara's "dying tones are in that other tongue, / To which some strange remembrance wildly clung" (2.444–5). This "strange remembrance" is only known to Kaled. Byron continues,

> And once as Kaled's answering accents ceas'd,
> Rose Lara's hand, and pointed to the *East*:
> Whether (as then the breaking sun from high
> Rolled back the clouds) the morrow caught his eye,
> Or that 'twas chance, or some remembered scene
> That raised his arm to point where such had been
> (2.444, 466–71; emphasis added)

Lara's gesturing towards the "East" marks a direction for his "mental net" of subjectivity, offering one explicit trajectory for the Byronic subject within this cosmopolitan imaginary.

This gestural "East" serves as the defining motif through which Byron expresses Lara's geographical past and, in effect, "Eastern" subject formation. In response, Kaled "[s]carce … seem'd to know, but turned away" (2.472–3). In doing so, Byron points to obscurity as a type of cosmopolitan impulse. Kaled, ambiguously signified in terms of race, ethnicity, gender/sex, reinforces the idea of an over-expanded poetic subjectivity but also, as Byron reminds us, the previous tale's representation of Gulnare.[57] In addition to overexpansion, Kaled embodies, as Diego Saglia reminds us, "the most conspicuous signifier of otherness and textual marker of dislocation" in *Lara* (401). This dislocation discounts Byron's cosmopolitanism and resists the Eurocentric myth of Westernized modernity as equivalent to cultural progress.

This final "East" also illustrates the changing limits and concerns of Byron's poetic subjectivity. As a whole, *Lara* lacks the historiographical allusions, footnotes, and Orientalist staging of previous tales. This lack could imply Byron's turn away from previous Orientalist practice. This turn is reinforced by the equivocal and uneven setting in *Lara*. Not only is it a cosmopolitan or Orientalist imaginary, but it is also a bookended medieval dystopia. Through Lara's return home and the

---

57   In addition to overexpansion, Kaled embodies, according to Diego Saglia, "the most conspicuous signifier of otherness and textual marker of dislocation" in *Lara* (401). This dislocation not only discounts Byron's cosmopolitanism but also resists the Eurocentric myth of Westernized modernity and its equivalence with cultural esteem or progress.

transposed "Eastern" setting located in a feudal past, Byron de-familiarizes his poetic subjectivity into a category of its own alterity.[58]

"And Kaled—Lara—Ezzelin, are gone!": Concluding the Tales

In addition to illustrating cosmopolitan interests and the Westernized placement of the poetic subject, these four tales chronicle Byron's growing disenchantment with his personal and public identity. Although by 1813 Byron had risen to a celebrity level of literary success via the *Pilgrimage* and *The Giaour*, Byron generally did not think he was writing satisfactory poetry and found deficiency in poetry's "scale of intellect."[59] Byron writes in a November 1813 letter to Lady Byron, the month before *The Bride of Abydos* is published,

> I by no means rank poetry or poets high in the scale of intellect ... This may look like affectation, but it is my real opinion ... I prefer the talents of *action*—of war—or the Senate—of even of Science—to all the speculations of those mere dreamers of another existence ... and spectators of this. — —Apathy—disgust—& perhaps incapacity have rendered me now a mere spectator—. (*BLJ* 3: 179)

As "a mere spectator" of "the talents of *action*," Byron finds his own limitations and the limits of poetry as an intellectual and public project. Often, the representations and characters we find in these tales register this sense of "[a]pathy" "disgust" and "incapacity." Indeed, Byron's *Pilgrimage* and first four Eastern Tales are viewed not only by the public, but perhaps most intensely by Byron himself. As spectator and creator of these Eastern Tales, Byron expresses his personal reactions against provincial ties and his self-fashioning within the shifting norms of an increasingly transnational poetic space. This space valorizes expression and associates the popular with foreign places and past times—a poetic enterprise that can bely not only poetry's "scale of intellect" but also, I would argue, the scale of the individual poetic subject (*BLJ* 3: 179).[60]

Byron's move to larger ambits of individual subjectivity through the Eastern Tales is an early-career moment of Byron's aesthetic invention. Through this expansion, Byron reinforces a cosmopolitanism centered in the "West." This cosmopolitanism requires a counterpoint of global "Eastern" experience in order to individuate itself.

---

58   After *Lara*, John Murray anonymously published two more of Byron's verse tales, *The Siege of Corinth* and *Parisina*. They appeared in the same volume in February 1816, two months before Byron left England.

59   Byron enjoyed their popular reception, but he considered the Eastern Tales largely inferior works. He called *Lara* "too little narrative—and too metaphysical" (*BLJ* 4: 295).

60   Part of the tales' difficulty lies in their stereotypes of the "East" and the rise of Orientalism simultaneously with comparative studies in the wake of Sir William Jones's foundational work. In my book, *Romanticism and the Poetics of Orientation*, I discuss the intertwined genealogies of comparative studies and the lyric form in Romantic-era poetry.

In creating a textualized "East," Byron hazards an identity beyond the limits of one's nationality or place of origin—one that extends the poetic subject to unclear cultural and geographical signifiers. Studying these tales provides a unique opportunity to interrogate Byron's cosmopolitan impulses and how these very impulses gave way to his later cultural and ethnic repertoires. By expanding the poet's subjectivity beyond geographical borders, these tales represent the spirit of an era in which shifting global and cosmopolitan relations unsettled the limits and boundaries of poetic form and content.

ISSN 0301-7257 (print) 1757-0263 (online)

THE BYRON JOURNAL

Volume 48 No. 1 2020

Isaac Robert Cruikshank, illustration to a pirated edition of *Don Juan* I–V (Smeeton, 1826) © The British Library Board.

Publishing scholarly articles and notes on news of significant events and conferences in the Byron year, as well as reviewing all major works on the poet.

A journal devoted to all aspects of Lord Byron's writings and life, and on related topics.

LIVERPOOL
UNIVERSITY PRESS
FOUNDED 1899

www.liverpooluniversitypress.co.uk
SUBSCRIBE FOLLOW @LIVUNIPRESS PUBLISH

https://doi.org/10.3828/eir.2020.27.2.7

The Battle of the Bards: Canings and Unchivalrous Masculinity

William D. Brewer
Appalachian State University

On 18 August 1800, the rotund and asthmatic sixty-two-year-old poetic satirist John Wolcot (1738–1819)—who wrote under the pseudonym Peter Pindar—entered John Wright's London bookshop at 169 Piccadilly Street and approached William Gifford (1756–1826), a diminutive forty-four-year-old Tory satirist with a deformed back. Gifford was seated and reading a newspaper. According to Wolcot, after he confirmed Gifford's identity and vigorously caned him, he was disarmed by the shop's occupants. He then pummeled Gifford with his fists but was pinioned by "by a tall *Frenchman*" named Jean-Gabriel Peltier, which enabled Gifford to cudgel Wolcot in his turn.[1] Other reports insisted, however, that Gifford averted injury by deftly wresting Wolcot's cane away from him and used it to beat his feeble opponent, who was thrown ingloriously out into the street. Conflicting accounts of the fracas appeared in newspapers throughout England, a postscript appended to the third edition of Gifford's *Epistle to Peter Pindar* (1800), a long footnote to Wolcot's *Out at Last! Or, The Fallen Minister* (1801), Alexander Geddes's poem *Bardomachia; or, The Battle of the Bards* (1800), and Thomas Dermody's *The Battle of the Bards. An Heroic Poem* (1800).

Eight years before the battle of the bards, another verse satirist, John Williams (1754–1818), whose pen-name was Anthony Pasquin, was brutally caned—either in a street near Haymarket Theatre or in a coffee-house—by the actor Captain George Wathen (1762–1849).[2] Williams had allegedly insulted Wathen. As in the case of the Wolcot-Gifford rencontre, contradictory descriptions of the fray appeared in the periodical press, and the combatants claimed that whereas they had conducted themselves honorably and courageously, their opponents had behaved cowardly and ungentlemanly. According to Williams, Wathen and another actor, William Barrymore, viciously caned and kicked him, but despite having lost the use of his right arm, he cudgeled them valiantly.[3] For his part, Wathen insisted that "the cane [...] was the proper chastisement for [Williams's] insolence, his boasting, and his

---

1   *Lloyd's Evening Post*, 22–5 August 1800.
2   Philip H. Highfill, Jr., Kalman A. Burnim, and Edward A. Langhans, eds, *A Biographical Dictionary of Actors, Actresses, Musicians, Dancers, Managers & Other Stage Personnel in London, 1660–1800*, 16 vols (Carbondale and Edwardsville: Southern Illinois University Press, 1973–93), 1:356, 15:292.
3   Highfill, Jr., et al., eds, 1:356; John Williams, "A Declaration," *The Oracle*, 19 July 1792.

affectation of courage."⁴ He dismissed as a joke his adversary's "DECLARATION" in *The Oracle* that as "a man of spirit," Williams was ready to give anyone offended by his writings "satisfaction."⁵ Gifford, who detested Williams's anti-royalist satires, mocked his injuries in a note to his poem *The Baviad* (1791). Both the battle of the bards and the Williams-Wathen caning resulted in vicious and inconclusive print duels in which the aggrieved bourgeois antagonists asserted their manhoods and gentlemanly statuses with ad hominem rhetoric. None of them seems to have seriously considered fighting a formal duel or taking legal action to protect his reputation.

In this essay, I examine the Piccadilly bookshop imbroglio and the ensuing debate over it within the contexts of Romantic-era notions of chivalric masculinity and the class symbolism of caning versus dueling. According to Tim Fulford, in the late eighteenth and early nineteenth centuries, "Chivalric manhood did not die; it was relocated in the middle classes."⁶ Cultural constructions of chivalric masculinity during this period were, as Michèle Cohen has shown, shifting and "sometimes contradictory."⁷ Cohen maintains that British men no longer conflated chivalry with politeness, which became associated with France and effeminacy, and observes that "because it was possible to attribute different meanings to chivalry[,] [...] it could be, and was, appropriated by politically and culturally diverse writers, politicians, poets, essayists, and artists, ranging from [Edmund] Burke's 'political lament for the *ancien régime* in France' to liberal or radical writers in the 1790s."⁸ Like Williams and Wathen, Wolcot, a physician turned anti-ministerial poet, and Gifford, an anti-Jacobin who had risen from the working class, felt entitled to deploy chivalric rhetoric and physical violence and claimed that they were fearlessly defending their honor and reputation. After their brawl, Gifford treasured Wolcot's confiscated cane as if it were a tournament trophy. They shared with the combative early nineteenth-century journalists examined by Richard Cronin a penchant for attacking "the 'personalities,' [...] the personal appearance and the private lives of [their opponents]" and "a need violently to insist that print was so intimately connected with the fleshly body of its author that the offences of the one might properly be visited upon the other."⁹ For them, chivalric manliness did

---

4   *The World (1787)*, 20 July 1792.
5   John Williams, "A Declaration," *The Oracle*, 19 July 1792, 1.
6   Tim Fulford, *Romanticism and Masculinity: Gender, Politics and Poetics in the Writings of Burke, Coleridge, Cobbett, Wordsworth, De Quincey and Hazlitt* (Houndmills and New York: Macmillan and St. Martin's, 1999), 9.
7   Michèle Cohen, "'Manners' Make the Man: Politeness, Chivalry, and the Construction of Masculinity, 1750–1830," *Journal of British Studies* 44 (2005): 315. For an illuminating discussion of gentlemanly masculinities during the late Georgian era, see William Stafford, "Gentlemanly Masculinities Represented by the Late Georgian *Gentleman's Magazine*," *History* 93 (2008): 47–68.
8   Cohen, 320, 315, and David Duff, *Romance and Revolution: Shelley and the Politics of Genre* (Cambridge: Cambridge University Press, 1994), 21. Cohen remarks that "Politeness in men can be associated with wimpishness, but chivalry is always manly" (320n59).
9   Richard Cronin, *Paper Pellets: British Literary Culture after Waterloo* (Oxford: Oxford University Press, 2010), 39, 153.

not necessarily entail politeness and decorum, and although Wolcot had composed neo-Burkean sentimental poems lamenting Queen Marie Antoinette's tragic plight, both he and Gifford had unchivalrously insulted women in their satires.[10] Borrowing terms from the sociologist Erving Goffman, I contend that Wolcot and Gifford regarded their fracas as a mutually "*fateful*" "*character contest*" that each one hoped would uphold his own gentlemanly status and display his strong, respectable, and masculine character while exposing his antagonist's impotence, ignobility, and unmanliness.[11] Neither man could, however, control "the characterological outcome of the contest"[12] as it played out in the contemporary media, and the resulting controversy harmed their reputations. Whereas Noah Heringman states that "William Gifford proved to be the greatest knight of [...] all [of Wolcot's critics] in his chastisement of the dragon Peter Pindar,"[13] I will argue that Gifford and Wolcot both failed in their attempts to perform chivalric manhood credibly: they profoundly miscalculated how their uncodified behavior and emasculatory rhetoric would be received. No one seems to have been persuaded by Wolcot's contention that because he was a gentleman and Gifford had once been a cobbler's apprentice, the chivalric code authorized Wolcot to cane rather than duel his parvenu adversary, and observers denounced Gifford's insinuations that Wolcot was a pederast, declaring them unmanly. Wolcot's and Gifford's gentility claims were further compromised by the fact that they profited from their writings; as Cronin notes, "the old notion that those who wrote for money forfeited their gentlemanly status [...] survived into the early decades of the nineteenth century," even "amongst professional journalists."[14] For example, "having conceived the high-minded idea that a gentleman should not take money for his poetry like a Grub Street hack," Lord Byron gave Robert Charles Dallas the copyright to *Childe Harold's Pilgrimage*, Cantos 1 and 2.[15] As evinced in

---

10   See Wolcot's "The Captive Queen. *The Lines are supposed to be spoken by a Friend of the unfortunate* ANTOINETTE" and "THE QUEEN OF FRANCE TO HER CHILDREN, *Just before her Execution*. An Elegiac Ballad," in *Pindariana; or, Peter's Portfolio* (London: J. Walker, J. Bell, J. Ladley, and Mr. Jeffrey, 1794), 63–4, 171–2.

11   Erving Goffman, *Interaction Ritual: Essays on Face-to-Face Behavior* (Garden City: Anchor Books, 1967), 164, 240 (emphases in original).

12   Goffman, 245.

13   Noah Heringman, "'Manlius to Peter Pindar': Satire, Patriotism, and Masculinity in the 1790s," *Romanticism and Patriotism: Nation, Empire, Bodies, Rhetoric*, ed. Orrin N. C. Wang, Romantic Circles Praxis Series (May 2006), https://romantic-circles.org/praxis/patriotism/heringman/heringman_essay.html, par. 18.

14   Cronin, 128. For Wolcot, authorship proved extremely lucrative; see Benjamin Colbert, "Petrio-Pindarics: John Wolcot and the Romantics," *European Romantic Review* 16.3 (2005): 311.

15   Leslie A. Marchand, *Byron: A Portrait* (Chicago: University of Chicago Press, 1970), 102. As a young man, Robert Southey also believed that gentleman-authors should not be motivated by profit. Nick Groom has shown that in Southey's 1799 dispute with Sir Herbert Croft over editing Thomas Chatterton's works, Southey established his gentlemanliness by disclaiming any proceeds from the edition and excoriated the ungentlemanly behavior of the upper-class Croft, who made a great deal of money from publishing some of Chatterton's letters in his novel *Love and Madness: A Story Too True* (1780) without obtaining the consent of the owners of the originals, Chatterton's mother and sister, and without adequately compensating them. Nick Groom, "Love and Madness: Southey Editing

the British print media, the cultural responses to the battle of the bards shed light on the inchoate embourgeoisement and evolving conceptions of chivalric masculinity during the Romantic period.

Wolcot and Gifford differed sharply in their political outlooks, moral attitudes, and approaches to satire. While Wolcot repudiated Thomas Paine's revolutionary ideology, he identified himself as a populist—a "POET OF THE PEOPLE"—and satirized King George III, William Pitt, and other members of the ruling class.[16] Gifford was a staunch Tory, a defender of the monarchy, and an anti-reformist. Whereas Wolcot courted controversy with his bawdy verses and "religious irreverence," Gifford represented himself as a protector of morality and religion, and in his postscript to the third edition of *Epistle to Peter Pindar*, he expressed horror at Wolcot's ribaldry, blasphemy, and alleged atheism.[17] As Gary Dyer has observed, "while Gifford and [Thomas James] Mathias personified the revived Juvenalian mode in satire, Wolcot's tradition split into two branches: Horatian and Radical."[18] Gifford adopted a hostile and abusive tone in his satires, which wield sarcasm, invective, and ad hominem attacks against their targets. Unlike his model Juvenal, who trained his fire on the dead, Gifford mercilessly lashed the living.[19] His most famous poems, *The Baviad* and *The Maeviad* (1795), skewered the "effeminate" Della Cruscan School of poetry and embodied the "Satiric masculinity" traditionally associated with Juvenal.[20] In contrast, Wolcot's Horatian satires were witty, humorous, playful, and ironic. His mock epic masterpiece *The Lousiad, an Heroi-Comic Poem* (1785–95) poked fun at King George's horror upon discovering a louse on his plate and mimicked his famous verbal tics:

Chatterton," in *Robert Southey and the Contexts of English Romanticism* (Aldershot and Burlington: Ashgate, 2006), 25–30.

16   See Peter Pindar, *More Money! Or, Odes of Instruction to Mr. Pitt: With a Variety of Other Choice Matters* (London: J. Evans, 1792): "*Though by no means an advocate for* Mr. Payne's [*sic*] *violent system of Revolution, I am too much the* POET OF THE PEOPLE, *not to sing for a* Reformation" (n. pag.). Also see *Odes to Mr. Paine, Author of "Rights of Man;" on the Intended Celebration of the Downfall of the French Empire, by a Set of British Democrates, on the Fourteenth of July* (London: J. Evans, 1791): "SON of Sedition, daring PAINE, / Whilst speech endues thy treason tongue, / Bid the roof ring with damned song, / And EREBUS [darkness] echo back the strain" (7).

17   Heringman, par. 16. Benjamin Colbert notes that Wolcot's "bawdy allusions and coarse bachelor habits set off the Reevesite watchdogs" (313). For Gifford's moral denunciation of Wolcot, see *Epistle to Peter Pindar*, 3rd ed. (London: J. Wright, 1800), 44–5.

18   Gary Dyer, *British Satire and the Politics of Style, 1789–1832* (Cambridge: Cambridge University Press, 1997), 37.

19   As William Barr notes, in Juvenal's first Satire, he "promise[s] to limit himself to attacks on the dead [...] References to living individuals by name [in *The Satires*], disparaging or otherwise, are in fact rare, and the people named serve for the most part as examples, not targets." William Barr, Introduction, *The Satires*, by Juvenal, trans. Niall Rudd, ed. William Barr (Oxford: Oxford University Press, 1991), xix.

20   *The Satirist, or Monthly Meteor* praised Gifford for his attacks on "The effeminate conceits of the Della Crusca school." "Living Satirists" (London: Samuel Tipper, 1808), 1: 123; for a discussion of Juvenalian "Satiric masculinity," see Dyer, 53.

"How, how? what, what?—what's that, what's that?" he cries,
With rapid accent, and with staring eyes—
"Look there, look there—what's got into my house?
"A louse, God bless us! louse, louse, louse, louse, louse."[21]

During the politically-fraught French Revolutionary period, Wolcot's satires of George III and Pitt became increasingly controversial and aroused the ire of anti-Jacobin writers such as Mathias, who accused Peter Pindar of "revil[ing], and h[o]ld[ing] up to scorn, every master principle by which government and society are maintained."[22] The public debate over the battle of the bards focused, however, not on Wolcot's and Gifford's politics but on their maladroit performances of masculine gender roles.

Having operated throughout his writing career within the largely anonymous and pseudonymous world of topical satire, in which satirists launched attacks with virtual impunity, often behind the masks of literary personas, Wolcot seems to have imagined he could literalize the metaphorical cudgel of satire without incurring serious consequences. He and Gifford blurred—perhaps elided—the distinctions between satirical and physical aggression, persona and actual person, and they failed to foresee that their behavior would be seen as inappropriate. They had not even met each other before their brawl; their mutual animus was based solely on their publications. In fact, Wolcot had to ask Gifford to identify himself in the bookshop, and Gifford only discovered after the fracas that Peter Pindar was the persona of a man named John Wolcot. Their feud originated in Wolcot's mistaken belief that Gifford had authored two attacks against him: a denunciation of Pindar's "rooted depravity and malignity of heart" in a footnote to Mathias's anonymously published *The Pursuits of Literature* (1794–9) and a scathing, ad hominem review of Wolcot's *Nil Admirari; or, A Smile at a Bishop* (1799) in *The Anti-Jacobin Review and Magazine* (November 1799), then edited by *John* Gifford (a pseudonym adopted by John Richards Green).[23] Wolcot retaliated against his supposed antagonist in a postscript to *Lord Auckland's Triumph: Or the Death of Crim. Con.* (1800), in which he ridiculed Gifford's humble background as a cobbler, accused him of being Lord Grosvenor's pimp, labeled him a "literary swindler," "scoundrel," and "villain," and declared that "a fellow with the form of the letter Z, who publicly attacks an unfortunate woman for a disorder of which the DIVINE BEING is the sole author, is little less than a demon and a fool."[24]

The "unfortunate woman" whom Wolcot chivalrously defended was his friend Mary Robinson, a disabled poet, novelist, and former mistress of the Prince of

---

21   Peter Pindar, *The Lousiad, an Heroi-Comic Poem*, Canto 1, new ed. (London: George Goulding and John Walker, 1793), 19.

22   Thomas James Mathias, *The Pursuits of Literature, or What You Will. A Satirical Poem in Dialogue. With Notes. Part the First*, 2nd ed. (London: J. Owen, 1976), 7.

23   Mathias, 7.

24   Peter Pindar, *Lord Auckland's Triumph: Or the Death of Crim. Con. A Pair of Prophetic Odes* (London: W. and C. Spilsbury, 1800), 50.

Wales. Gifford had sneered at her lameness in *The Baviad*, in which "Robinson forget[s] her state, and move[s] / On crutches tow'rds the grave, to 'Light o' Love'" (ll. 27–8), and hinted in a footnote that she had had an abortion: "Light o' Love! that's a tune that goes *without a burden*."[25] In the postscript to *Lord Auckland's Triumph*, Wolcot depicted Gifford as an anti-chivalric monster who had attacked a woman in distress, and Leigh Hunt and William Hazlitt subsequently echoed his excoriation of Gifford's "unmanly" treatment of Robinson.[26] But whereas in the postscript Wolcot assumed the role of Robinson's champion, in his previous satires he had traduced her and other women. His comparison of Robinson to the Athenian courtesan Thais in *More Lyric Odes to the Royal Academicians* (1783) horrified Samuel Taylor Coleridge, and his *Nil Admirari* lampooned the poet Hannah More as an overrated writer, plagiarist, and prude who scribbled "pages of puerile vanity and intellectual imbecillity [*sic*]."[27] As his contemporary readers knew, when it came to venerating women, Wolcot was far from a knight-errant.

Rather than apologizing for his vicious attack on Robinson, Gifford doubled down. His suggestion in *Epistle to Peter Pindar* that Peter might like to "hire one hobbling strumpet to [his] arms" may have been aimed at her.[28] In the first and second editions of *Epistle*, he responded to Wolcot's defense of Robinson by disingenuously denying that he had maligned her "disorder" and then warning her to stay out of his "way":

> It is probable that neither Peter nor the lady understood a syllable of what they read; otherwise they must have seen, that no reflection was intended on her "disorder," whoever was the cause of it, but on the improper use she made of what the pious Peter is pleased to call a divine visitation. But a word with you, "Sappho." This is the second time you have wantonly fallen in my way. I humbly beseech you to let it be the last. I have sometimes more plainness then patience, and may be tempted to say what we shall both be sorry for. You rely, it may be, on the prowess of your flash-man—so, I think they call Peter—you might rely with infinitely more wisdom, on a broken reed: for, to tell

25   *The Baviad, A Paraphrastic Imitation of the First Satire of Persius* (London: R. Faulder, 1791), 9, 8n; see Sarah Gristwood, *Perdita: Royal Mistress, Writer, Romantic* (London: Bantam, 2005), 204–5. Gifford adapts lines from Shakespeare's *The Two Gentlemen of Verona* (1.2.80–2) and *Much Ado about Nothing* (3.4.44–5).

26   See Leigh Hunt, *The Companion* (London: Hunt and Clarke, 1828), 376; Hunt, *The Autobiography of Leigh Hunt*, new ed. (London: Smith, Elder, & Co., 1891), 194; and William Hazlitt, *The Spirit of the Age: or Contemporary Portraits*, 2nd ed. (London: Henry Colburn, 1825), 259, 272.

27   Peter Pindar, *More Lyric Odes, to the Royal Academicians* (London: T. Egerton, 1783), 18; *Nil Admirari; or, A Smile at a Bishop* (London: West and Hughes, 1799), 5. Coleridge wrote to Robinson's daughter that his "flesh creeps at [Peter Pindar's] name!!" and denounced him for "call[ing] an infamous & mercenary Strumpet '*the Mrs Robinson of Greece*.'" *The Collected Letters of Samuel Taylor Coleridge: 1801–1806*, ed. Earl Leslie Griggs, vol. 2 (Oxford: Clarendon Press, 1956), 905–6.

28   *Epistle to Peter Pindar*, 3rd ed., 23, line 28.

you a secret, which I care not how soon you repeat to Peter, I fear him even less than I do you[.][29]

"Flash-man" was slang for "A whore's bully," or a bouncer in a brothel.[30] Addressing Robinson by her erotically-charged pseudonym, Sappho, Gifford implied that her behavior toward him had been wanton and that she was a prostitute whose impotent bully was frailer than "a broken reed." He suggested that since she was a demirep consorting with a flash-man, he did not owe her the respect due to a lady, and thus his insults and threat were not unchivalrous. Gifford may, however, have decided later that his defamatory warning to Robinson detracted from the gentlemanly image he wanted to project: he removed it from the third edition of *Epistle to Peter Pindar*.

In the poets' vitriolic print battle, Gifford's attacks against Wolcot in the three editions of *Epistle to Peter Pindar*, published in quick succession by his ally Wright, landed many more blows than Wolcot's salvos against Gifford in *Lord Auckland's Triumph*, his 22 August 1800 letter to the *Oracle*, and his footnote to *Out at Last!*. Presenting himself as a counterpuncher who did not start the quarrel but was determined to "reduce[] Peter to his proper level," Gifford weaponized and progressively expanded his allegations, threatening to exact further retribution with the cane of satire: "I will make no attack;" he wrote, "but prompt, and signal, and 'ten-fold' retribution shall be sure to follow every blow [Peter] aims at me."[31] He sought to emasculate Pindar/Wolcot verbally and brand him as a pederast while emphasizing his own chivalric manliness, rectitude, courage, and defiance. Gifford dubbed Peter an "impotent dotard" and "an impotent scribbler" and "fearlessly pronounced [him] a most despicable poltroon; a white-liver'd, crest-fallen, and thrice beaten coward."[32] Describing Peter as "feeble from years, more feeble from vice" and "whimpering like a sick girl," Gifford alleged that his adversary was too incapacitated either to duel or assassinate an enemy: Peter's "drunkenness and debauchery" rendered his "hands too unsteady for a pistol, and too feeble for a stiletto."[33]

In the inflammatory postscript to the second edition of *Epistle* that instigated the bookshop scuffle, Gifford ramped up his attack by repeatedly intimating that Peter was a pederast, likening him to the openly homosexual Peribomius in Juvenal's second satire.[34] Whereas in the first edition Gifford contented himself with

---

29   *Epistle to Peter Pindar*, 1st ed. (London: J. Wright, 1800), 28.
30   See Captain Grose, *Lexicon Balatronicum: A Dictionary of Buckish Slang, Univ. Wit, and Pickpocket Eloquence* (London: C. Chappel, 1811), n. pag.
31   *Epistle to Peter Pindar*, 3rd ed., 53, 37n. In a footnote in the 3rd edition of *Epistle*, Gifford explains "the asperity of" his attack on Peter Pindar: "I have borne [Pindar's] abuse for more than fifteen years, without a complaining word; [...] I never gave him, either directly, or indirectly, the slightest cause for offence; and [...] I now declare [...] that, till the present moment, I never wrote a syllable concerning him in the whole course of my life" (20).
32   *Epistle to Peter Pindar*, 3rd ed., 11, 19, 39.
33   *Epistle to Peter Pindar*, 3rd ed., 36, 52, 39.
34   Juvenal, *Satire*, 2:15–19.

suggesting in a footnote that Peter should use Peribomius rather than Pindar as his pseudonym, in the second edition he referred to Peter as "our modern Peribomius" and as "honest Peribomius," noting their *"perfect* similarity of character" and remarking that while Pindar may continue to fulminate about "'coblers and pimps,'" "catamites, I suppose, he will think proper to omit."[35] He also mentioned that he had received "a letter from an Officer who assisted in kicking [Peter] out of Maker Camp for his scandalous indecencies."[36] The second and third editions of *Epistle* included a facsimile of a scribbled, unsigned letter, purportedly from Peter Pindar, that threatened Gifford, his "boyish supporters," and "the Tyrant Pitt" with vengence and declared that "the Bird Cage Walk," which runs to Buckingham Palace, "shall have its reward" [FIGURE 1].[37] Dismissing the letter as the product of Peter's "dotage,"[38] Gifford sarcastically invited Peter to write an ode to the Bird-Cage Walk, which, according to the eighteenth-century memoirist George Parker (1732–1800), was the "chief place" in London where sodomites met each other.[39] In the third edition, Gifford omitted the allusion to "catamites" and reprinted an allegation published in *The Times* in March 1789 that Peter Pindar, while gathering materials for *The Lousiad* and other satires, had been "caught" engaging in "disloyal and ******** intercourse" with "a *Kitchen Rat* at Buckingham House [...] in a trap [...] in the *Bird-Cage-Walk.*"[40] Having provided newspaper evidence of Peter's dalliance with a royal scullion, Gifford "thr[e]w [him]self, with *manly* confidence, on the unsophisticated sense of [his] country."[41] His Juvenalian rhetoric in *Epistle* was unsparingly harsh, emasculatory, and homophobic, and he proved to be much more adept at character assassination than his more Horatian foe, whose retaliatory footnote in *Out at Last!* is only about four pages long and who apparently abandoned his plan to lambaste Gifford in a poem that his publisher advertised as *A Little Lash at a Little Liar; or, A Cut at the Cobler.*[42] Wolcot preferred to lash Gifford with acerbic prose rather than neo-Horatian verse.

---

35   *Epistle to Peter Pindar*, 1st ed. (London: J. Wright, 1800), 13n; *Epistle to Peter Pindar*, 2nd ed. (London: J. Wright, 1800), 43, 40. In the second edition of *Epistle*, Gifford's quotation from a poem written in French implicitly associated Pindar with the French musician and burlesque writer Charles Coypeau d'Assoucy (1605–77) (referred to as "Monsieur D'Assouci" in the poem), who traveled throughout France and Italy with boys who served as his musical pages (40). See François Le Coigneux de Bachaumont, *Œvres de Chapelle et de Bachaumont* (Paris: Quillau, 1755), 282. The quotation was not included in the third edition.

36   *Epistle to Peter Pindar*, 3rd ed., 20.

37   *Epistle to Peter Pindar*, 2nd ed., n. pag.

38   *Epistle to Peter Pindar*, 2nd ed., 40.

39   George Parker, *A View of Society and Manners in High and Low Life; Being the Adventures in England, Ireland, Scotland, Wales, France, &c. of Mr. G. Parker*, 2 vols (London: Printed for the Author, 1781), 2:87.

40   *Epistle to Peter Pindar*, 3rd ed., 41; *The Times*, 19 March 1789.

41   *Epistle to Peter Pindar*, 3rd ed., 42 (emphasis added).

42   Wolcot's publisher advertised Peter Pindar's *A Little Lash at a Little Liar* in *The Morning Chronicle (1770)*, 7 August 1800, claiming that it would be "Speedily [...] published"; see also *The Morning Chronicle (1770)*, 19 August 1800.

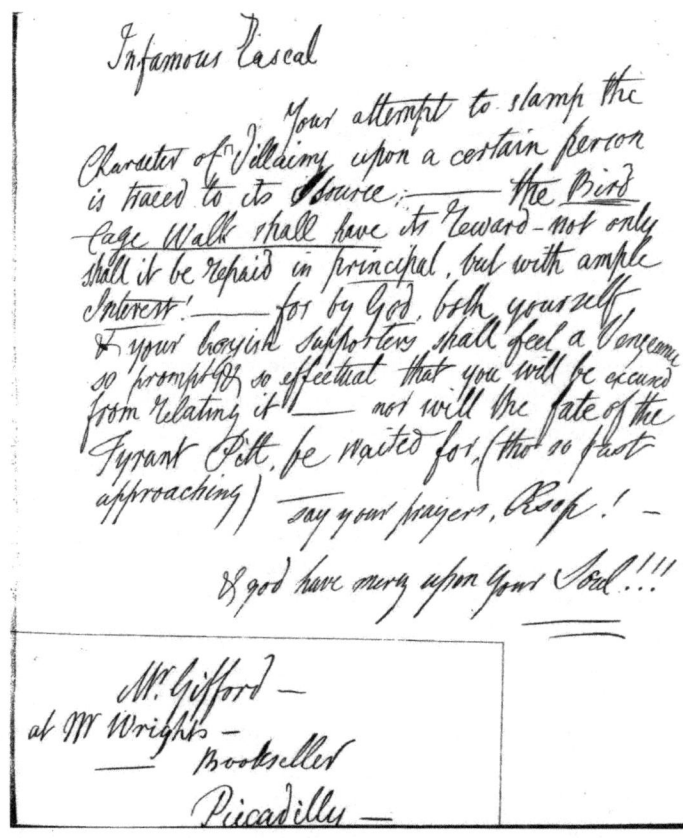

FIGURE I: Facsimile letter published in the 2nd and 3rd editions of William Gifford's *Epistle to Peter Pindar* (1800).

Throughout *Epistle*, Gifford portrayed himself as manly, fearless, and resolute. In the introduction, he indignantly rebuffed the suggestion that he feared Pindar: "This was an idea which had never struck me, and which, indeed, I could not hear with patience [...] *Fear!* No, never in my humblest moments did so unworthy a thought possess me as that of being suspected of fearing so feeble, so odious, so contemptible, so utterly despicable an object as Peter Pindar!"[43] In his poem, written before the bookshop incident, Gifford dared Pindar to attack him:

43   *Epistle to Peter Pindar*, 3rd ed., 12.

[...] dip thy trembling hands in coward gore, [...]
But touch not ME, or, to thy peril know,
I give no easy conquest to the foe.
Come then, all filth, all venom as thou art,
Rage in thy eye, and rancor in thy heart,
Come with thy boasted arms, spite, malice, lies,
Smut, scandal, execrations, blasphemies;
I brave 'em all. Lo, here I fix my stand,
And dare the utmost of thy tongue and hand,
Prepar'd each threat to baffle, or to spurn,
Each blow with ten-fold vigour to return.—[44]

Wolcot's incursion into Wright's bookshop provided Gifford with the opportunity to demonstrate his knightly prowess. By representing Wolcot/Pindar as an "impotent dotard," however, Gifford made his alleged victory over him seem easy and thus unheroic. He allowed it to appear as though he had disarmed and severely beaten a weak old man rather than a credible assailant. While Gifford melodramatically described the attack as an "attempt at assassination"—undercutting his claim that Wolcot was too feeble to pose a threat—and Wright accused Wolcot of intending "to maim and disable, Mr. GIFFARD [sic]," Wolcot never faced legal charges, and most commentators regarded his behavior as risible rather than criminal.[45]

Heringman has suggested that "the paradox 'hysterical masculinity' may help to elucidate" Gifford's caning of Wolcot and his "punishing" castigation of him in *Epistle to Peter Pindar*.[46] The same phrase can be applied to Wolcot's hyperaggressive response to Gifford's implicit pederasty charges. Whereas Wolcot was risk-taking and combative in his satires, he tended to be timid and nonconfrontational in person; his atypically violent behavior in Wright's bookshop seems to have been driven by hysterical fury. According to his fellow Cornishman Richard Polwhele, Wolcot was "of a very timid disposition in conversation, soon overawed by a superior character, or checked by the dread of corporal correction from the person he despised," and the writer and editor John Taylor was "often [...] surprised, as [Wolcot] was really a timid man, how he could venture to take such freedoms, not only with the royal character, but with many of the upper ranks."[47] While residing in Cornwall, Wolcot provoked a challenge from General William Macarmick, but looking out his bedroom window on the morning of the duel, he was unnerved by the sight of the General grimly striding across the field of honor with "a brace of pistols in his hand, altogether a sight not calculated to add to a man's personal

---

44   *Epistle to Peter Pindar*, 1st ed., 27, lines 53–64.
45   *Epistle to Peter Pindar*, 3rd ed., 60; *The Morning Post*, 23 August 1800.
46   Heringman, par. 19.
47   Tom Girtin, *Doctor with Two Aunts: A Biography of Peter Pindar* (London: Hutchinson, 1959), 80; John Taylor, *Records of My Life* (New York: J. & J. Harper, 1833), 364.

courage in a cold morning."[48] He avoided the duel with an effusive apology. Henry Rosewarne, a target of Wolcot's lampoons, reportedly pulled him by the nose and caned him in Truro's Market Place.[49] Despite, however, his aversion to physical confrontation, the intense rage that Wolcot felt against the writer who had publicly depicted him as a sodomite impelled him to burst into the hostile environment of a Tory bookshop—the headquarters of the ultra-Tory *Anti-Jacobin Review and Magazine* was upstairs—and either cudgel or attempt to cudgel one of its leading lights.[50] As V. G. Kiernan indicates, "Gentlemen must be ready to fight, but with decorum and dignity, not like the noisy plebeians they had too often resembled."[51] Even a peer could be deemed ungenteel if he failed to maintain his composure while defending his honor: the notorious hothead Lord Camelford (1775–1804), who ignited a scandal in 1796 by fiercely caning the explorer Captain George Vancouver in a London street, "was on the whole little regretted" by his male contemporaries after he died at the age of 29 from a gunshot wound sustained in a duel.[52] In Wolcot's frenetic attempt to avenge libels and establish Gifford's social inferiority, he did not exhibit the self-possession expected of a gentleman.

Why did Wolcot not sue Gifford for libel? Perhaps he was discouraged from doing so by John Williams's ill-fated 1798 libel suit against one of the publishers of Gifford's *The Baviad*, at the conclusion of which the judge declared that "the author of the Baviad has acted a very meritorious part in exposing [Williams]" as an "unprincipled and mercenary wretch[]," and "*The Jury, without a moment's hesitation, non-suited the Plaintiff.*"[53] Heavily in debt from his legal expenses, Williams fled to America, and in the introduction to *Epistle to Peter Pindar*, Gifford congratulated himself for "the ridding of this country of [Williams]."[54] Taking a libeler to court is, of course, a decidedly *un*chivalrous mode of seeking redress: a lawsuit does not allow the aggrieved party to demonstrate his physical courage by placing himself in bodily peril, nor does it offer him the opportunity to vent his fury by punishing the offender manually. As Wolcot knew, however, many aristocrats, the traditional

---

48   Cyrus Redding, *Fifty Years' Recollections, Literary and Personal*, 3 vols (London: Charles J. Skeet, 1858), 1:272.

49   Girtin, 80.

50   On the close relationship between Wright's bookshop and the two *Anti-Jacobin* journals, see David Fallon, "Piccadilly Booksellers and Conservative Sociability," in *Sociable Places: Locating Culture in Romantic-Period Britain*, ed. Kevin Gilmartin (Cambridge: Cambridge University Press, 2017), 73, 76–7.

51   V. G. Kiernan, *The Duel in European History: Honour and the Reign of Aristocracy* (Oxford: Oxford University Press, 1988), 136.

52   Nikolai Tolstoy, *The Half-Mad Lord: Thomas Pitt, 2nd Lord Camelford (1775–1804)* (New York: Holt, Rinehart and Winston, 1978), 188.

53   "Proceedings on the Trial of Robert Faulder, Bookseller, (*One of* FORTY *against whom Actions were brought for selling the Baviad*) FOR PUBLISHING A LIBEL ON JOHN WILLIAMS, Alias ANTHONY PASQUIN, ESQ.," in *The Baviad, and Mæviad*, by William Gifford, 6th ed. (London: J. Wright, 1800), 187–8.

54   *Epistle to Peter Pindar*, 3rd ed., 13.

embodiments of chivalric masculinity, took legal action against libelers. For instance, Lord Lonsdale, whom Wolcot pilloried in *A Commiserating Epistle to James Lowther, Earl of Lonsdale and Lowther* (1791), initiated a libel action against him.[55]

Instead of suing Gifford for libel, challenging him to a duel, or lambasting him yet again in print, Wolcot chose to assault him with a cane because he believed that caning would symbolically brand the former cobbler his social inferior. In a letter that he tossed into the bookshop after the brawl, he wrote:

> As there are certain expressions that require only a little of the severity of satire by way of a corrective, so there are others of so malignant a nature as to demand a horsewhip instead of words. Had you possessed something more of the human form, I should have treated you as a *Man*; but as things are, you must be content to be whipped as a malicious Monkey.[56]

Whereas dueling etiquette required challengers to have letters submitted to their prospective opponents *before* the conflict, in his anti-duel, Wolcot reversed the procedure, delivering the letter *after* the rencontre. As a former physician and clergyman, Wolcot considered himself a gentleman and socially above Gifford, who had been a cobbler's apprentice. Eighteenth- and early nineteenth-century antagonists who agreed to meet each other in a clandestine formal duel implicitly acknowledged each other's gentility. As Cronin explains, "Issuing a challenge and administering a whipping are both of them aggressive acts, but the duelling pistol acknowledges the right of the man who is challenged to be admitted within the same social circles as the challenger, whereas the horsewhip [or cane] violently proclaims its victim's social inferiority. Hence, looked at in another way, the two acts are antithetical. To issue a challenge, however unfortunate the consequences may be, is in some sense an act of inclusion."[57] By assaulting his archenemy in a shop, with a cane, and without a prior challenge, Wolcot publicly declared that Gifford was not a gentleman and hence his inferior. In 1792, Captain Wathen's savage caning of Williams and his scornful dismissal of William's published offer to provide "satisfaction" delivered a similar message.

---

55 Colbert, 314.
56 *The Oracle and the Daily Advertiser*, 22 August 1800; reprinted in *Epistle to Peter Pindar*, 3rd ed., 59.
57 Cronin, 123. Like their British counterparts, late eighteenth- and early nineteenth-century American gentlemen interpreted canings as insults. As Joanne Freeman informs us, "everyone understood the implicit meaning of a caning—a sound beating about the head and shoulders with a cane. Because only equals were supposed to duel, canings displayed the victim's inferior status. A caning was no symbolic smack; gentlemen often purchased 'stout hickory' walking sticks deliberately for this purpose. [...] The implied insult of both canings and nose-tweakings was the same; not only were they profoundly humiliating public assaults, they were badges of inferiority as well." Joanne Freeman, *Affairs of Honor: National Politics in the New Republic* (New Haven: Yale University Press, 2001), 172.

In the report of the affray submitted by Gifford's confederate Wright, however, it is Wolcot rather than Gifford who is aligned with the working class: "After PETER was turned into the street, the spectacle of his bleeding head attracted a mob of hackney coachmen, watermen, paviours, &c. to whom he told his lamentable case."[58] David Fallon notes that "Wright associate[d] Pindar with the mob, an illegitimate and heterogeneous outdoor public in contrast to the gentlemen of the shop, although Piccadilly was a fashionable aristocratic street."[59] Moreover, in Wolcot's narrative of the brawl, his assertion that he "had recourse to the fist" undermined his claim to gentlemanly status: "renew[ing] the combat à la Mendoza" was behaving like a proletarian.[60] Applying a boxing term to Wolcot, whose blood splattered the shop window, Taylor wrote that his friend had "lost some claret."[61] As Robert B. Shoemaker informs us, "Among the lower classes, boxing (without gloves) was the preferred method of settling disputes, but this was deemed unsuitable for gentlemen."[62] Wolcot went after Gifford with a stick to confirm his opponent's social inferiority, but descriptions of Wolcot's comportment cast doubt on his own gentility. According to the *Albion and Evening Advertiser*, Wolcot lost his hat in the scuffle, "which was thrown out to him; but [Gifford] kept possession of [Wolcot's] cane as a trophy of his triumph."[63] While Wright linked Wolcot to the rabble, Gifford sought to play the role of a victorious knight glorying in his tournament trophy.

The "characterological outcome" of Gifford's verbal and physical attacks on Wolcot was also equivocal: critics deplored his ungentlemanly insults and hints that Wolcot was a pederast, and Wolcot's claim that Gifford, Wright, customers, shopmen, and a tall Frenchman had ignobly ganged up on him was widely circulated. A review of *Epistle to Peter Pindar* in *The Critical Review* complained that

> the greater part of the Introduction, almost the whole of the Epistle, and more particularly the *anonymous* Postscript, are compounded of such low and Billingsgate abuse, such outrageous contempt of all that decorum which should ever regulate the language of the gentleman and the scholar, and which the public has at all times a right to expect from those who appeal to its judicature—such dark inuendos [*sic*], and unsupported hints of the foulest of vices, that we have seldom seen their superior, and trust we shall never again be forced to witness their equal.[64]

---

58   *The Morning Post*, 23 August 1800.
59   Fallon, 82.
60   *The Oracle and the Daily Advertiser*, 22 August 1800; *Lloyd's Evening Post*, 18–20 August 1800. Daniel Mendoza (1765?–1836), who had been employed by tradesmen in his youth, was an acclaimed prizefighter (*ODNB*).
61   Taylor, 390.
62   Robert B. Shoemaker, "The Taming of the Duel: Masculinity, Honour and Ritual Violence in London, 1660–1800," *The Historical Journal* 45 (2002): 529.
63   *Albion and Evening Advertiser*, 19 August 1800.
64   Review of *Epistle to Peter Pindar*, *The Critical Review; or, Annals of Literature*, vol. 30 (London: S. Hamilton, 1800), 475.

Similarly, the editor of the *Dramatic Censor*, Thomas Dutton, "took Gifford severely to task for accusing John Wolcot of 'a crime at which human nature shuddered [...] He brings no proof and knows it to be false.'"[65] *The Morning Chronicle* and *The General Evening Post* criticized Gifford for making "an allusion" in the second edition of *Epistle* "of a kind too gross for decency to record," and the *Lloyd's Evening Post* denounced Gifford's "gross and abominable libel on the character of a man, [which], unless well-founded, may, in a great degree, justify the abrupt conduct of Peter Pindar."[66] A writer for *The Morning Post* asserted that no man could feel safe "in the company of" such a malicious libeler:

> Peter Pindar seems to have been stimulated to this step by the foulest and falsest libels, on the part of Mr. Giffard [*sic*], that ever issued from the English press. Mr. Giffard charged a crime upon Peter, from a suspicion of which the world never altogether exempts those who charge it. The whole of a long and most scurrilous attack in a pamphlet might have been palliated by the previous attacks of Peter; but no provocation on earth can palliate so infamous a calumny as that alluded to; and Mr. Giffard will probably feel the effects of it throughout life, since no man of prudence and character can be safe in the company of one who falsely makes such charges.[67]

In homophobic Georgian England, in which sodomy was a capital offense and men convicted of attempting to commit sodomy could be maimed or killed in the pillory, allegations of pederasty had potentially lethal ramifications.[68] For a number of commentators, Gifford's insinuations that Wolcot had committed such a "foul" crime were anti-chivalric, mendacious, indecent, and reckless.

Not surprisingly, Wolcot portrayed his behavior in the bookshop as justifiable and gallant and complained that Gifford was the unchivalrous beneficiary of his supporters' interventions. In a 22 August 1800 letter to *The Oracle*, Wolcot asserted that after he began caning Gifford, "several people" came to the miscreant's rescue:

> WRIGHT and his customers, and his shopmen, immediately surrounded me, and wrested the cane from my hand. I then had recourse to the

---

65   Girtin, 207.

66   *The Morning Chronicle (1770)*, 19 August 1800; *The General Evening Post*, 16–19 August 1800; *Lloyd's Evening Post*, 18–20 August 1800. Also see the *Hereford Journal*, 27 August 1800.

67   *The Morning Post*, 19 August 1800.

68   See Louis Crompton, *Byron and Greek Love: Homophobia in 19th-Century England* (Berkeley and Los Angeles: University of California Press, 1985), 18, 21, 31. In *Homosexuality & Civilization*, Crompton writes that in the eighteenth century, "Abuse of sodomites became a way for Englishmen to affirm their manhood and allay any suspicions about their own sexuality" (Cambridge: The Belknap Press of Harvard University, 2003), 461. Heringman discusses Gifford's libels within the contexts of "the legal status of sodomy allegations, [...] and [...] the currency of sodomy in political rhetoric" (para. 20).

fist—and really was doing ample and *easy* justice to my cause—when I found my hands all on a sudden confined behind me particularly by a tall *Frenchman*. Upon this GYFFORD [*sic*] had time to turn round, and with his own stick—a large one too—struck me several blows on the head. I was then hustled out of the shop, and the door was locked against me [...] I [...] retired to the house of a friend for about an hour, and returned to WRIGHT's shop to *finish* the affair; but the door was still locked, and GYFFORD, I believe, in the house. Some of the shopmen came forward, and told me that I should not enter—upon which I desired them to inform GYFFORD, that wherever I met him, he might depend on every castigation due to his calumny—that Society ought to be purged of such a dangerous pest [...] GYFFORD has given out as a matter of triumph that he possesses my cane, and that he means to preserve it as a trophy. Let me recommend an Inscription for it—"The CANE of JUSTICE, *with which I* WILLIAM GYFFORD, *late Cobler of Ashburton*, have been soundly drubbed for my Infamy."[69]

According to Wolcot's account, he sallied forth into the Anti-Jacobin stronghold to exact righteous vengeance but was overcome by Gifford's numerous allies. Wright, his customers, and his shopmen teamed up to disarm him, and he was then pinioned by Peltier, a towering Frenchman, who enabled the previously helpless Gifford to dishonorably beat his defenseless foe with a large stick. Wolcot's attempt "to *finish* the affair" and purge society "of such a dangerous pest" was thwarted by a locked door, protective shopmen, and Gifford's cowardly refusal to continue the fight. To underscore Gifford's non-gentlemanly status and the appropriateness of caning rather than dueling him, Wolcot reminded his readers that his foe had once been a cobbler.

Wright, who stipulated that he was not in his shop during the incident, responded to Wolcot's letter in a statement first published in *The Morning Post*. Basing his hearsay evidence on information provided by two unidentified witnesses, presumably his shopmen, Wright wrote that Gifford's response to Wolcot's sudden attack was dexterous, calm, and chivalric:

> [Peter Pindar] raised a stick he had brought for the purpose, and levelled a blow at [Gifford's] head, with all his force. Mr. GIFFARD [*sic*] fortunately caught the stick in his left hand, and, quitting his chair, wrested it instantly from the cowardly assassin, and gave him two severe blows with it; one of which made a dreadful impression on Peter's scull [*sic*]. Mr. GIFFARD had raised the stick to strike him a third time; but seeing one of the gentlemen present about to collar the wretch, he desisted, and coolly said, "Turn him out of the shop."

---

69   *The Oracle and the Daily Advertiser*, 22 August 1800.

Insisting that Gifford conducted himself with gentlemanly coolness, Wright remarked that the vanquished Peter sought medical treatment and then "slunk home, 'With his crack'd pate be-plaister's and be-patch'd, / Like an old paper lantern!'"[70] Fallon explains that "The quotation comes from the *Bacchides* of Plautus, in a note to Gifford's translation of Juvenal, and refers to a pederastic teacher, obliquely reinforcing the original libel."[71] Whereas Wolcot described Gifford as initially passive and then, after Wolcot's hands were seized, opportunistically aggressive, Wright portrayed his associate as a gallant combatant with lightning reflexes who disarmed, battered, and then contemptuously dismissed his craven and pederastic assailant. Unlike Gifford, Wolcot had no allies in the shop who could testify on his behalf, and he did not have a proficient spokesperson and rapid-fire publisher like Wright.

Gifford and Wright's claim that Gifford subjected his inept foe to a humiliating defeat has been accepted as accurate by Gifford's biographer Roy Benjamin Clark and Wolcot's biographer Tom Girtin, and Heringman concludes that "the most widely credited account suggests that Gifford beat Wolcot bloody with his own stick."[72] Contemporaneous articles and satires responding to the fracas did not, however, reach a consensus about what transpired. While some periodicals privileged Wolcot's description of the rencontre, others favored Wright's pro-Gifford report, and many others adopted an agnostic approach and printed both versions of the event.[73] Although Gifford was a fervent Tory and Wolcot was anti-ministerial, critiques of their brawl focused on the inappropriateness of their conduct and language rather than on their politics. *The Morning Post* decried both Gifford's "infamous [...] calumny" and Wolcot's "unmanly" allusions to "the obscurity and humbleness of Mr. Giffard's [*sic*] early life" and concluded that "These gentlemen would have acted wisely had they fought by deputy, and sent their Muses along into the field of battle. They might have expected that a combat of private character would but bespatter both, by holding both up to the derision of the world."[74] The satirical poems *The Battle of the Bards*, by Thomas Dermody (1775–1802), and *Bardomachia*, by Alexander Geddes (1737–1802), roughly follow Wolcot's account, in which he struck first and was then brutally beaten by multiple assailants. Dermody was an alcoholic Irish poet who

---

70   *The Morning Post*, 23 August 1800.

71   Fallon, 82.

72   Roy Benjamin Clark, *William Gifford: Tory Satirist, Critic, and Editor* (New York: Russell & Russell, 1958), 19; Girtin, 202; Heringman, par. 18. Without identifying his source(s), Robert L. Vales states that Wolcot "struck [Gifford] on the head with his cane. Gifford wrestled the stick from Wolcot's hand, drubbed him at least twice, and pushed Wolcot out of the bookshop door, making him lose his hat, cane, wig, and some blood." *Peter Pindar (John Wolcot)* (New York: Twayne, 1973), 21.

73   Commenting on Wolcot's description of the fracas, an article in *Lloyd's Evening Post* (18–20 August 1800) concludes: "This statement, we have reason to believe, is very near the truth." A similar piece ran in the *Hereford Journal* (27 August 1800). Publications that printed both sides of the story included *The Morning Post* (23 August 1800); *The Times* (26 August 1800); *Bell's Weekly Messenger* (24 August 1800); *Albion and Evening Advertiser* (19 August 1800); and *Whitehall Evening Post (1770)* (21–3 August 1800).

74   *The Morning Post*, 19 August 1800.

occasionally frequented Wright's shop;[75] Geddes was a Scottish Catholic priest and biblical scholar. In Dermody's lampoon, Peter cudgels Gifford's "impenetrable" and "hollow" skull and is then overwhelmed by Gifford, "Associate fists," the "coward cuffs" of "PARTHIAN PRENTICES," and an "eminently tall, [...] bony FRENCHMAN."[76] In Geddes's *Bardomachia*, Peter canes "Mæviades" (Gifford) but is disarmed in mock-heroic fashion by Phœbus Apollo, pinioned by the "gigantic PELTIER," and attacked by Castor and Pollux, who assume "the shape of shop-men." The poem condemns Mæviades's subsequent caning of the defenseless Peter: "[he] raised the stick, and laid it hard / On the bald hind-head of the routed bard. / Ignoble deed!— Who wounds a vanquish'd foe? / Cowards alone such wanton valour show."[77] In the concluding lines, Geddes stresses the futility of Wolcot and Gifford's "bloody war":

> Both, with disgrace,
> Become the scorn and laughter of the place;
> The mocking-stock of even the populace.
> Who, for their sake, a tear of pity sheds?
> Or spreads a plaister for their batter'd heads?
> Even broth-bards regardless pass along,
> And in loud laughter join the vulgar throng.[78]

Similarly, an anonymous burlesque titled *Peter and Æsop, a St. Giles's Eclogue* (1800) concludes that the satirists' scuffle rendered both of them ridiculous: "To the surrounding mob these men of worth / Afforded inextinguishable mirth."[79] For many observers, the bookshop brawl turned both Wolcot and Gifford into laughingstocks, and by resorting to libel and billingsgate, they tarnished their literary reputations.

Unlike the formal duel, which was meant to resolve gentlemen's honor disputes, canings did not preclude further provocations and violence. After their brawl, however, Gifford and Wolcot confined themselves to an exchange of print fusillades. Gifford delivered his parting shot in the third edition of *Epistle to Peter Pindar*, and Wolcot replied in a footnote to *Out at Last!*:

> On the appearance of this *Gentlemen's* last *lying* publication, which was in some measure answered by the *argumentum baculinum* [argument to the cudgel], I entertained thoughts of a *formal execution* of the felon,

75 Fallon, 76.
76 Thomas Dermody, *The Battle of the Bards. An Heroic Poem. In Two Cantos. The Author Mauritius Moonshine* (London: Lackington, Allen, and Co., 1800), ll. 109–10, 144, 146–8, 150. Somewhat obscurely, Dermody alludes to "Such odious hints as [Peter's] own Manhood stain" (line 121), possibly alluding to the pederasty allegation.
77 Andrew Geddes, *Bardomachia: or, The Battle of the Bards* (London: J. Crowder, 1800), 12–13.
78 Geddes, 15–16.
79 Anon., *Peter and Æsop, a St. Giles's Eclogue* (London: Murray and Highley, J. Harding, V. Griffith, 1800), lines 219–20, 31.

in a solemn poetical epistle; but, on reflexion, thinking him beneath the dignity of such an exhibition, I determined to *hang him* in a *note*.

> For, should the *Muse's* satire bid him die,
> The GODDESS really *guillotines a Fly*.[80]

Wolcot reprised and expanded his charges against Gifford, critiqued the bombast, unevenness, unoriginality, and "verbose pomposity" of his verse, and reiterated his contention that Gifford had been "cudgeled in [...] WRIGHT's shop [...] for his atrocious calumnies."[81] Somewhat belatedly, Wolcot sought to vindicate his poetic acumen as well as his chivalric manhood. Perhaps due to the publicity generated by the bardomachia, *Out at Last!* went through six editions in England and was also published in Philadelphia.

In his memoir, Taylor credited himself with ending the feud between Wolcot and Gifford: "I [...] explained to Dr. Wolcot his mistake in confounding the two Giffords, and attacking the wrong one. When the matter was understood by both parties, all enmity was at an end. I succeeded in making them send amicable inquiries as to the health of each other, which I conveyed with pleasure."[82] As Clark observes, however, "neither satirist withdrew his charges; each continued to republish them in subsequent editions of his work,"[83] and Wolcot's friend William Godwin gave the name Gifford to the Iago-like villain of his novel *Fleetwood* (1805). There was no cessation of hostilities on the publishing front. Writing sixteen years after the bookshop affray, William Cobbett contended that Gifford's "insinuati[on] that [Wolcot] had been guilty of an attempt, at least, to commit *unnatural crimes* [...]was reprobated by every man of every party" and that "the reprobation of [Gifford's] conduct towards Peter Pindar became so loud and so general, that [his] employers took the alarm. Fearing to be confounded with [Gifford], they hastened to withdraw their names from the list of subscribers to the Poetry of the Anti-Jacobin."[84] According to Cobbett, after *The Poetry of the Anti-Jacobin* fiasco, a chastened Gifford "avoided to engage *openly* in political contests, and ha[s], ever since, been spitting out anonymous venom."[85] Cobbett's assertion that Wright's proposed edition of *The Poetry of the Anti-Jacobin* was aborted solely because of Gifford's insinuations ignores other possible causes of its demise: Fallon points out that George Canning and John Hookham Frere "withdrew their names from the subscription and encouraged others to do so" after Wright and James Gillray refused to let them inspect Gillray's "*ad hominem* caricatures," and Wright, who was declared

---

80   Peter Pindar, *Out at Last! Or, The Fallen Minister*, 6th ed. (London: West and Hughes, 1801), 13n.
81   *Out at Last!*, 13n, 11n.
82   Taylor, 390.
83   Clark, 21.
84   William Cobbett, "To MR. WILLIAM GIFFORD, EDITOR OF THE QUARTERLY REVIEW," *Cobbett's Weekly Political Register* 30 (New York: H. Cobbett and G. S. Oldfield, 1816), 334–5.
85   Cobbett, 335.

bankrupt in 1802, "seems to have financially overstretched himself."[86] But while Cobbett appears to have exaggerated the public's disapprobation of Gifford's conduct, the furor over *Epistle to Peter Pindar* suggests that Gifford's defamatory attack injured his as well as Wolcot's reputation. Like Wolcot's attempt to delegitimize Gifford's claim of gentlemanly status with a cane, Gifford's sexual libels backfired.

Steven E. Jones writes that "Satire shares with dueling conventional rituals of mutual verbal aggression." But whereas satires and meetings on the field of honor are "both codified ritual practices,"[87] a surprise cane attack in a bookstore is not. As Cronin points out in his discussion of fatal duels fought in 1821 and 1822 that "had their origin in [periodical] writing," "The duel was [...] seductive for a brief period because it was an institution that allowed literary men at once to express towards one another a murderous aggression and to ratify each on the other's behalf the right of professional writers to gentlemanly status."[88] If Wolcot had formally challenged Gifford and they had scrupulously adhered to dueling protocols and their meeting had been publicized, the print media might have validated their performances of chivalric masculinity. They were, however, socially insecure satirists, temperamentally averse to the displays of mutual respect and politeness demanded by the code duello, and they refused to regard each other as equals: Wolcot cast Gifford as a lowly cobbler, a monkey only fit to be whipped, and Gifford portrayed Peter Pindar—the literary avatar whom he belatedly discovered was a person named Wolcot—as much less than a man. They were intent on demolishing, not ratifying, each other's gentlemanly status. When they turned from stylized rhetorical assaults to unritualized physical violence, their behavior came across as farcical and reprehensible. Contemporary commentators thought that poets were meant to compose well-crafted verse, not brutally club each other. By contrast, Captain Wathen's caning of the satirist Williams provoked relatively little controversy: Wathen had seen action during the siege of Gibraltar and had been "a *gentleman*-actor with [...] Lord Barrymore," and thus, unlike Wolcot, he fit the part of a virile man of honor wreaking vengeance on an insulter.[89] Although Gifford's adherents proclaimed him the victor of the battle of the bards, neither man performed chivalric masculinity convincingly. The poets' "mutual abuse," *The Morning Post* lamented, "does neither of them honour; and, what is worse, it tends to dishonour literature."[90] Their conduct was not only unchivalrous, it was also unbardlike.

---

86 Fallon, 84.
87 Steven E. Jones, *Shelley's Satire: Violence, Exhortation, and Authority* (DeKalb: Northern Illinois University Press, 1994), 75.
88 Cronin, 10, 16.
89 *The Thespian Dictionary; or, Dramatic Biography of the Eighteenth Century* (London: T. Hurst, 1802), n. pag., emphasis in the original.
90 *The Morning Post*, 19 August 1800. The author of *Peter and Æsop* wrote: "To [Peter Pindar's and Gifford's] talents, [...] I am ready to do homage; but I must ever express my disgust, or be permitted, at least, to laugh, at the miserable, not to say beastly, use these irritable men make of such valuable endowments" (vi).

https://doi.org/10.3828/eir.2020.27.2.8

Index